The Practical Financial Manager

The CFO's Resource
for Maximizing Cash Flows

Lawrence M. Krackov, MBA, JD
Assistant Treasurer, CBS Inc.

Surendra K. Kaushik, PhD
Professor of Finance, Pace University

New York Institute of Finance

Krackov, Lawrence M.
    The practical financial manager.

    Bibliography: p.
    Includes index.
    1. Corporations--Finance. 2. Capital market.
I. Kaushik, S. K., 1944-   . II. Title.
HG4026.K697 1988   658.1'5   88-5317
ISBN 0-13-689373-2

This publication is designed to provide accurate and authoritative information in regard to the subject matter covered. It is sold with the understanding that the publisher is not engaged in rendering legal, accounting, or other professional service. If legal advice or other expert assistance is required, the services of a competent professional person should be sought.

From a Declaration of Principles Jointly Adopted by
a Committee of the American Bar Association and a
Committee of Publishers and Associations

Printed in the United States of America
10 9 8 7 6 5 4 3 2 1

New York Institute of Finance
(NYIF Corp.)
70 Pine Street
New York, NY 10270-0003

*To Susan Krackov, Helena Kaushik,
and the rest of our families
for sacrificing their time with us.*

*LMK
SKK*

Contents

CHAPTER 3
Buzzwords versus Financial Analysis: The Defense Never Rests

CHAPTER 4
Residual Values and Their Importance: The End Justifies the Means

CHAPTER 5
What Are the Relevant Variable Costs for Different Decisions?

Contents

Contents

Contents

Preface

The financial analysis techniques that work in the ''real world'' are usually only extrapolations of the *basics* of finance. The ones that do not work generally either ignore the basics or add more sophistication than a given project warrants or that the corporate budget can bear.

Although the basics are usually included in the early courses in college, many practitioners tend to get away from them. For example, the proper application of present value and cost-of-capital concepts should go a long way even in such specialized areas as acquisitions, corporate restructuring, and/or international finance. Yet when we fail to apply the basics, we are likely to make two kinds of mistakes.

The first is regressing to the ''old-fashioned,'' ''seat-of-the-pants'' type of business decision making. The second is becoming fair game for those consultants, bankers, and other financial services agents who sell math, buzzwords, and the promise of windfall profits. If we are lucky, our losses are limited to the amount of their fees. If not, we wind up running counter to the basics, ultimately increasing our capital costs and/or reducing our present values.

The point of this book is therefore that many a financial blunder can be avoided and cash flows maximized by applying the fundamentals of financial analysis. Beyond that, one can maintain a consistent clarity of analysis in the most complex of financial transactions simply by stressing the basics first and only then turning to more sophisticated quantitative methods.

Toward that end, the authors have more than 17 years of experience in the financial functions of several Fortune 500 companies, as well as in practical seminars, training programs, and college-level courses. In addition to being grounded in day-to-day experience, the material in this book has been successfully class-tested at two major universities in the following areas and courses:

Finance Area

- General Finance
- Managerial Finance
- Cases in Finance
- Principles of Investment
- Security Analysis & Portfolio Management

Multifunctional Business Area

- Mergers and Acquisitions

Accounting Area

- Cost Accounting & Control

Law

- Business Law

Such extensive practical experience and educational testing bring into sharp focus the lessons to be learned from the misapplications and the failures to apply sound analytical principles. Yet such failures are surprisingly pervasive in both business and academia.

The prospective reader of this book is anyone who has even minimal training or experience in finance and who is responsible for profitably supervising financial transactions. The corporate executive is perhaps the most obvious reader. Others are the small business owner/operator, corporate financial manager, commercial and investment banker, venture capitalist, capital market investor, financial consultant, and others who meet the financial needs of a corporate clientele. The book can also be used fruitfully in college courses in financial management, at both the graduate and undergraduate levels.

It should also be appropriate for reading assignments connected with professional seminars or conferences and corporate executive training programs.

The text is organized to respond to three questions of finance:

1. In which assets and businesses should funds be invested?
2. What is the cheapest source of funds in the capital markets?
3. What is the optimal mix of funds, in terms of debt versus equity, and what is the related impact on dividends?

All three questions are, of course, related to one primary aim of corporate finance: The optimal allocation of resources or funds, from creditors and equity investors, among assets and businesses within the corporate sector, and control of corporate management.

To assist financial managers in their daily pursuit of this aim, the text demonstrates application of fundamentals to a wide range of subfunctions, such as mergers and acquisitions, international finance, corporate restructurings, capital budgeting, and others. Each section contains actual examples of misapplications, showing how the same type of misapplication can occur in different areas of analysis.

While it does not offer perfect solutions to all the financial bloopers, the book approaches a wide range of issues with a financial fundamentals perspective. By doing so, we hope to reveal the inherent riskiness of the overly complex approaches often touted about in the business world. Inasmuch as the intention is to raise issues, we hope to receive heavy feedback from readers. All comments from executives, students, professors, and general readers are most welcome.

LMK
SKK

Acknowledgments

The authors are thankful to Scott Marden and Alan Rabinowitz for their professional evaluation of the manuscript and encouragement; Rebecca Taylor for secretarial and editorial help; Virat Rattanataymee for research assistance and word processing; and Fred Dahl, Director of Publishing, along with Jeanmarie Brusati at the New York Institute of Finance for the most efficient, professional, and courteous way to sign up and publish this book.

PART I

INVESTMENT ANALYSIS AND EVALUATION

CHAPTER 1

Price/Earnings
and Other Rapid-Valuation Ratios

Understanding Misleading Multiples

How many times have you heard that a company was trading at ten times earnings, two times book value, or even one and one-half times sales? In reality, this is simply not true! These are figures of speech. Businesses and assets trade at and are purchased for dollars or dollar equivalents, not multiples.

The Correct Use of Multiples

Businesses have a certain level of earnings and sales on their income statement along with net assets on their balance sheet. This is considered their *book value* under accounting principles. When the dollar purchase price for that business is divided by one of these three other factors, this yields a mathematical ratio or *multiple*. Of course, if we divided the stock price by the age of the owner's oldest son, this would also produce a ratio or multiple. These multiples must be derived in a way that indicates worth or value, not just an arbitrary factor.

Cash flow is basis of value. Stock price levels are a function of profitability and risk related to the profits and other cash-flow factors, including the present and future investments required to obtain those profits. Risk includes both the risk of not obtaining the expected cash flows from operations and the risk connected with the capital structure (as we will discuss in Chapter 20). Risk may result in higher debt leverage which causes one's net income, after fixed interest payments, to become much more volatile than operating profits. The total market value of a company, therefore, should merely be the value of the firm's projected cash flows discounted back to their present value, with the level of the discount rate set to account for the degree of overall risk.

But what about individual shareholder stock prices? Well, the value of individual shares should obviously be the present value of cash flows to the shareholder, such as dividends and proceeds from stock sold for capital gains. The value or selling price of the capital gains stock sales, however, is merely the value of the future dividends to the new shareholder. The present value or present stock price, therefore, is merely the present value of the future stream of dividends in perpetuity.

Price = Dividends/(Discount rate* − Growth rate for dividends)

This formula is merely the mathematical flip-side of the ever popular cost-of-equity formula.

Cost-of-equity % = (Dividends/Price) + Growth rate of dividends

If stock prices are a function of dividends paid forever in the future, they should be equal to the net cash flow generated forever in the future. The amounts retained and invested, whether needed or not, have already been subtracted from net cash flow, as well as from the dividends paid. So stock prices or the value of a company are merely the present value of future cash flows of the business, accounting for the risk or volatility of these cash flows.

Is this a big surprise? This is merely the first of many basic financial principles that we will rediscover in this book.

Comparing Multiples of Different Companies

In addition to the general misleading concept that businesses are valued at multiples of earnings, book value, sales, and so on, there is

*Cost-of-equity %.

still another misleading concept concerning the use of multiples. Multiples are often erroneously used in the interpretation of performance trends for one company or in comparing performance levels for two companies.

Back in 1977, when DuPont's price/earnings multiple jumped over the prior year's level and challenged the leader, Dow, it was merely a function of a very poor earnings performance, not a good one as many people would expect. DuPont's stock price actually dropped, but not nearly as much as earnings, because the market knew some rebound in the company's future performance was likely. Yet, Dow's high price/earnings level was attributable to further rapid-growth prospects following a rapid-growth, high-profitability performance record in earlier years. This was a 180-degree opposite reason for a similar price/earnings ratio level.

There have also been many rapid-growth performers with very low price/earnings ratios. This is a logical result of the market feeling that most of the growth has already been attained. In other words, you must look at specific factors before you can even tell whether a high or low P/E is a sign of success or failure.

And of course, let's not forget the risk or volatility of earnings attributable to operating factors and/or the degree of debt leverage. Higher risk means future earnings levels could easily fall below expectations at any time. The value of such a risky business, therefore, should be lower compared to the value based on its current earnings level.

Entertainment companies, popular book publishers, toy businesses, and similar operations are good examples of both concepts. They can grow quickly to become highly profitable after one or two hit films, records, books, toys, and so on. Yet, since these are "hit" businesses, the market will be asking what great money maker is next in line and what are the assurances that it will really be more or equally successful to provide continued earnings stability. The business, in other words, is to some extent only as good as the latest hit. Large numbers of new products, good distribution systems, and good promotional expertise for new products will help ameliorate the downside risk and negative effects on valuation. Nevertheless, these companies, therefore, often have lower price/earnings multiples than their current success or recent growth records would imply.

5

Multiples for Specific Industries

Ratios other than price/earnings (P/E) may be more relevant for specific industries. For example, price/sales for magazines or price/subscribers for cable operators are often cited in the trade press. We must not forget, however, that these ratios are also merely the result of prices, determined by the economic fundamentals, divided by the sales or subscriber levels.

Yet, there is usually a strong relationship between the level of earnings and the level of sales or subscribers and between the price/earnings level and the price/sales or price/subscriber level. At a given return on sales, there is obviously a direct relationship between the price/sales and the price/earnings ratios.

For a given revenue level per subscriber, which is a standard input in the cable industry, there is obviously a direct relationship between price per subscriber and price/sales. If one of the fundamental factors changes—i.e., a lower number of subscribers, but a higher revenue per subscriber—the present value calculations will generate a price that increases relative to the number of subscribers, but yields the same price/sales ratio.

Since sales or subscribers are so critical for magazine and cable operator businesses, they were chosen as the primary benchmarks by the trade press, entrepreneurs or deal makers in these industries. Yet, they not only have a relationship with the P/E ratios, but also greatly impact the profitability and net cash flows upon which present value prices are based. To the extent that some other factors significantly alter cash flows for a given company, the price—and the price/sales or price/subscribers—will be altered. If the factor is not identified by the market or an acquirer, will this not hold true? Bargains or overpriced companies can then be encountered in the marketplace.

Relations of Multiples to Acquisitions

The critical point is that the acquisition analysts first calculate a price range based upon a whole host of factors, emphasizing the present value of cash flows. Only then do they express these values as price/earnings, price/sales, or price/subscribers ratios. Thus, a low multiple is never a sure-fire sign of a bargain.

The deal makers among you readers may be ready to pounce on the preceding analysis. You may point to the many acquisition contract clauses that cite the actual price to be paid as some multiple, as opposed to a fixed dollar amount. Yet, these clauses are written only after the price valuation was determined and expressed as a ratio or multiple of one or more of the main underlying assumptions on which the price valuation calculations were based—such as sales or subscriber levels.

Many magazine acquisitions have had minimum and maximum price formulae tied to subscriber levels. Prices declined if subscriber levels declined below a target level. At a minimum level, the buyer has even had an option to abandon the deal, since an inadequate number of subscribers may indicate a fundamental weakness in the reader appeal. On the other hand, a maximum number of subscribers not only provided a maximum price (under a subscriber-related pricing formula), but also may have given the buyer an option to abandon the deal. The rationale is that certain subscription building promotions draw large numbers of new subscribers, but ones who are less likely to renew and less valuable to the advertiser. Also, they may have more copies due to them under newer, larger subscriptions, for which the seller has already obtained the proceeds and for which the buyer assumes the liability to supply the copies in the future.

Another area specifically related to both price/earnings ratios and acquisitions is usually misunderstood without careful study. The *post-acquisition P/E multiple* is often said to be merely a function of which P/E is applied to the combined earnings—that of the buyer, that of the seller, or both. Yet, it is merely a function of the value of the acquisition to the buyer, as perceived by the market, coupled with the pre-acquisition combined P/E ratio.

If the price paid equals the perceived value, if the stock of the buyer and seller were both traded on the stock market prior to the acquisition, if no synergies exist, and if no takeover speculation had affected either price, then the post-acquisition P/E level must necessarily be the original weighted average of the two pre-acquisition P/E multiples. For example:

Company A	Company B
Price per share = $10	Price per share = $20
Number of shares = 100 shares	Number of shares = 20 shares
Earnings per share = $2	Earnings per share = $1
P/E = 5x	P/E = 20x
Total market value = $1,000	Total market value = $400

- Post-Acquisition Combination

  Total market value = $1,400
  Total earnings = $220
  P/E = 6.36x

- Weighted Average P/E

  $$= [(5x) \times (200)] + [(20x) \times (20)] \div 220$$
  $$= 1,400 \div 220 = 6.36x$$

If, however, there are *synergies*, a *bargain purchase*, or both (causing the market to perceive the value to be greater to the buyer than the price he paid), then the post-acquisition P/E will be higher than the weighted average pre-acquisition P/E. In practice, then, even if a premium is paid over the stock market price, which gives the seller more than its share of the combined pre-acquisition market value, the stock price of the buyer need not decline because the post-acquisition P/E level can be raised.

In other words, as long as the seller's business or assets under buyer's control are worth the price paid—even if this price is more than the pre-acquisition, publicly-traded price of the seller—then the post-acquisition P/E can remain at or above the pre-acquisition weighted average P/E. Thus, the buyer's stock price can also be maintained, or even increased, despite the fact the seller received a premium for his stock. This is a classic case of how both parties can benefit in a good deal.

Please note that synergies in this case may include the new presence of the buyer's management expertise in a given field. Or the bargain aspects of the acquisition price may merely be the fact that in many cases publicly-traded companies are worth less than a controlled business or asset.

Asset Multiples

Now let's explore a price multiple that is often based upon assets rather than operating results, namely *price/book value* rather than P/E or price/sales. This valuation is merely representative of the valuation of the ongoing business dividend by the book value of its assets when a business is liquidated or sold in total or in any part. The *price/book ratio* also represents another set of fundamental values.

If a business is to be sold, the estimated sale proceeds are the returns to the investor as opposed to the ongoing cash flows from the income stream. The relationship of the market value of its assets—or of the business itself—to the historical accounting book values is the key. How much have the assets appreciated? This is the same phenomenon supporting the use of leveraged buyouts and leveraged takeovers that has become the latest craze. (We will discuss this subject further in Chapters 4 and 20.)

The type of industry of the business in question can also be a major factor. For example, real-estate assets are usually more valuable than their purchase prices; and the value after accumulated depreciation, shown on the balance sheet, is usually a fraction of total worth.

In addition to real-estate development companies, others requiring real-estate assets—especially if they are fungible and saleable, apart from the business itself—can have an equally high price/book value ratio. A perfect example is a restaurant/fast-food business. (This is discussed in more detail in Chapter 20 relating asset values to debt capacity.)

Summary and Conclusions

The economic fundamentals, derived from a business's income statement or balance sheet, can explain many of the types of price multiples used for various types of businesses. An analysis of the specific sets of income statements and balance sheets can also explain the comparison of the level of various multiples between any two companies. Yet the one point to remember is that the basic causal factors for the multiples are the same economic fundamentals that determine present value. This present value can be one of an ongoing business related to earnings, sales, or subscriber levels—or a business to be liquidated—related to asset book values.

CHAPTER 2

Capital and Its Management

A Capital Idea, or Is It?

We all know from economics, political science, history, and all those other areas describing our funny human institutions, that *capital* is one of the two major factors of production. The other is *labor*. All non-labor can be labeled *capital resources,* which are utilized by a business to generate a *profit return.*

Importance of Capital and Returns on Capital

As practical financial experts, we need to express capital in specific terms. Capital is merely that investment in business upon which an adequate return must be earned. This *return* must first be expressed as a percentage called the *return on capital.*

$$\text{Return on capital} = \text{Net profit/Capital invested}$$

That return must be compared with the comparable annual costs of investing in that capital. And what are the annual costs? Interest expenses, of course, in a comprehensive sense of the word.

Definition of Capital and Interest Costs

Capital is that investment in a business with annual interest expenses that must be equaled or exceeded by profit in order to provide an adequate return. Well, then isn't capital merely all the assets you invest in a business that remain on the balance sheet that have not yet been used up and expensed on the income statement (taking into account the fixed assets not yet depreciated and all the inventory not yet incorporated in the costs of goods sold)? The answer is no.

There are many businesses where there is little or no interest cost to provide the assets needed. Take a newsletter business, for example. The prepaid subscription proceeds will not only cover all the expenses, but if the business is profitable, the proceeds will often fund the minimal requirements for equipment, inventory, and leasehold improvements in the offices. The office building itself is often leased, and the printing is often done on a custom contract basis. Then, what is the capital invested in such a business? The answer is none or a negative number.

This is why using *return on assets* as the relevant financial criteria, or defining capital as total assets, would be a financial mistake. Return on capital should be measured against the real interest costs for the funds tied up in the business with such costs. Interest-free funds, therefore, should be subtracted from the total assets, so the higher return on the net amount left need be compared with only the company's average effective interest rates.

Before we proceed, let's define *interest costs* because we are using the term in a somewhat comprehensive sense. If funds are provided by a bank or other creditors, interest costs are easily identifiable as the designated interest rates charged. If funds are provided by shareholders or owners, or funds are retained in the business in lieu of paying dividends or other distributions to the shareholders/owners, then the interest costs are the returns required by the shareholders/owners. The weighted average of the two interest costs represents the cost of the capital funds invested. (For a more complete discussion of required returns related to capital costs, see Chapter 16.)

Thus, any funds provided by subscriber payments, suppliers' financing via receivables, and any other interest-free source of funds should not even be included in capital. Also, in reviewing the adequacy of profit returns from any business, only the return on capital funds with the added costs is relevant and not the lower return on total assets.

Capital on the Balance Sheet

Let's look at this concept on the balance sheet. The definition of capital discussed above is:

$$\text{Capital} = \text{Total assets} - \text{Interest-free liabilities}$$

On the right-hand side of the balance sheet, the same equation can be rewritten as:

$$\text{Capital} = \text{Interest-bearing liabilities} + \text{Owner's equity}$$

The first definition concentrates on capital investment requirements, but accounts for the interest-free liabilities as a reduction. The second definition concentrates on capital-fund sources. The two must always be equal. Look at the following figure, for example.

Figure 2-1. Balance Sheet Dissected

Assets	Liabilities/Equity
(1) Current Assets Fixed Assets	(2) Interest-Free Liabilities
	(3) Interest-Bearing Debt Equity
Total Assets	Total Liabilities and Equity

In this figure, Box #1 obviously equals Box #2 plus Box #3 because good balance sheets must balance. If capital equals Box #1 minus Box #2, then that must also be equal to Box #3. Box #3 really supplies funds at a cost of interest for Box #1 that are not supplied interest free from Box #2. And of course, to the extent interest-bearing debt and equity in Box #3 are required to fund asset requirements in Box #1, then only to that extent need a profit return be earned to cover costs and achieve an adequate return.

Since the main purpose of capital definitions is to review the adequacy of the returns versus costs, capital should always be defined as the market value of the equity and debt funds, because that is what the shareholders and banks have invested today. The weighted average costs calculated on market values will be the costs of new funds to be invested in new projects.

Management of Capital: Working Capital

With the definition and calculations of capital and capital costs now clear, it should be easy to understand how we manage or control capital to optimize the value of the firm.

First, investments in projects entailing increases in fixed assets and current assets that are not financed interest free must earn a return equal to or above the company's weighted average cost of capital. This obviously increases the value of the firm, which must mean the level of total capital is being optimized by the decision.

Second, managing capital entails an attempt to limit the amounts required for any given project. For example, specifications for new manufacturing plants should exclude all costs that cannot be justified on an incremental profit or policy basis. For working capital, however, minimization is not as clear cut. Even the definition of working capital is often a financial mistake. The old standby reads:

$$\text{Working capital} = \text{Current assets} - \text{Current liabilities}$$

Right? Wrong! You cannot automatically use an accounting formula for a financial concept. One of the best and most senior CPAs at an auditing firm reassured us that this is not heresy.

The correct definition flows from our prior discussion of capital. If total capital equals total assets minus interest-free liabilities, then the correct formula for working capital must be:

Working capital = Current assets − Interest-free liabilities

In other words, short-term debt, which is certainly a current liability, is not a reduction of capital but a component part of capital. It is part of interest-bearing debt in Box #3 on the right-hand side of the balance sheet.

This conclusion is well implemented by the rating agencies, such as S&P and Moody's, in their calculation of the relevant debt/capital ratios. *Short-term debt* is included in both the numerator and denominator. Many companies also utilize *commercial paper* as a primary source of debt capital financing and include it in debt and capital figures in the annual report.

In fact, textbooks and bankers talking about managing working capital by managing short-term debt are committing one of the most pervasive financial mistakes in practice. No wonder it takes years of experience to figure out a relatively basic concept. Short-term debt, such as bank-line drawdowns and commercial paper, are merely sources of capital funds. While they may be used as financing sources for only working capital for the sake of matching maturities (as discussed in Chapter 13), they are certainly not reductions in the amount of capital required to be financed at a cost.

One added nuance we have seen used is in the *zeroing out of any unplanned balance* on a daily basis at lock-box banks before the cash can be transferred to the concentration bank. Overdrafts can be treated as negative cash balances rather than debt, that offset the unplanned positive balance over the course of a month. Yet, the corporation may be faced with negotiating acceptance, or even de facto acceptance of this practice.

Now, if our goal is to minimize working capital, then we should not be concerned with short-term debt, but merely current assets and whatever interest-free liabilities are available. We should attempt to minimize the current assets and maximize the interest-free liabilities within limits.

15

Let's look at six accounts most commonly included in working capital management and how the goal of minimizing the level of working capital within constraints is implemented:

- *Cash and marketable securities* should be minimized by setting up bank overdraft facilities to fund your everyday needs. While these cash accounts earn a return, they have little to do with your business; and the returns are probably much lower than your cost of capital if liquidity is adequate to serve your everyday needs for cash. In the efficient cash management systems, therefore, zero-cash balances are a definite possibility.

  An example of such a system in practice would be to obtain funding requirements for all checks that will clear during that day from your main disbursement bank early in the morning. Then, all cash at your concentration bank can be transferred by wire to fund such disbursements or to be invested in marketable securities or the retirement of short-term debt, such as commercial paper. Ideally, there is always a shortage of cash, so that short-term debt, which is part of total capital, rises and falls whenever there are changes in disbursements needed for working capital. Thus, there is no ongoing balance of cash equivalents maintained; and capital is minimized to the level of requirements to support the business itself.

- *Receivables* also should be minimized, because they tie up money by delaying receipt from cash for revenues booked, even if the cost of goods sold have been paid. Yet, most businesses cannot compete without credit, and an analysis must be made of the cash flows lost from lost revenues, and/or the cost of discounts given to your customers for early payment, as compared with the cash flow obtained from reducing receivables.

- *Inventory* should also be minimized, but most businesses cannot run without a fair amount. It is usually needed either to support the production process or to generate customer sales. Remember, it's a lot tougher to sell a picture of a dream car than the car itself. Lost cash flows from production slowdown or lost sales must be compared with the cash freed up by reducing inventory levels.

- *Supplier payables* should be maximized to the point where your credit rating and supplier prices will not be adversely affected. It's nice to get the freebie financing, but if you do not pay your bills, you may certainly no longer be a valued customer.

- *Accrued salaries* should be maximized as another form of interest-free financing, but again, only up to a reasonable point. A paycheck every two weeks, or even every month, may work, but you certainly cannot pay your employees once a year—not if you plan to survive as a company.

- *Deferred revenues,* such as prepaid subscriptions, should be maximized. As discussed above, this is one of the best forms of interest-free financing that makes some magazines and newsletters yield infinite returns on capital.

To reiterate the obvious, the first three accounts are current assets, which are components of capital and working capital requirements. The next three are interest-free liabilities that are offsets to capital and working capital requirements or a reduction in capital financing sources needed.

In addition to the specific tradeoffs, the *current ratio* is one overall added constraint. In minimizing the current assets and maximizing interest-free liabilities classified as current (maturing in less than a year), your current ratio will obviously be reduced. This could become quite an important problem when you need financing or are concerned about a credit rating.

When you limit the magnitude of working capital by holding down receivables or inventory, you may also obtain some other benefits from reduced exposures. After all, if people owe you less, you have limited your chances for bad debt losses. Similarly, if inventory is kept low, less will remain after a selling season, and obsolescence risks should be reduced.

A Paradox: Minimize Capital, but Maximize Inflows

Finally, let's discuss a third financial mistake that is persuasive in understanding the management of capital. Should you minimize capital as outlined above, or should you maximize capital buildup from revenues, profits, and other proceeds flowing into capital assets?

Perhaps the answer is obvious to all of you, but it does appear to be a confusing paradox. We seek to maximize capital buildup, in terms of cash flow, and then seek to minimize the capital levels.

Cash management is probably the best example of the paradox. We should seek to minimize cash levels, even down to zero if bank overdrafts are available for daily fluctuation needs. Yet, our cash management system also seeks to maximize cash flows from customers through lock boxes, wire transfers, and so on.

What we are doing, therefore, is merely a two-step process. First, we maximize the liquidity of assets that are no longer needed to be tied up in capital through stringent capital budgeting for fixed assets, tight credit, and aggressive collections policies for receivables, and so on. Second, we use the liquidity of the resulting assets (cash and marketable securities) to remove the capital from the business. In practice, if cash and securities are controlled to a zero balance level, then the excess cash obtained from the other aspects of the business must be used to retire debt or to reduce equity through dividends and stock repurchases. In other words, the assets in the capital requirements of the business will be less and the capital financing supplied to the business will be reduced. Return on the capital will, therefore, increase and improve in comparison with the cost of the capital funds remaining.

Exceptions to the Rule

Now, before we conclude this chapter, we should address the many apparent exceptions to the *minimum-cash-and-capital philosophy* that we see in annual reports and press articles with respect to some of our largest and sophisticated corporations. Cash buildups, from both major divestitures and significant debt and equity issues, do generate huge "excess" cash and capital levels. Yet, these are often exceptions to the minimum-cash-and-capital approach, not a change in philosophy.

For example, many capital-intensive technological companies need liquidity available on short notice and at known interest rates to keep pace with product development requirements in their industries. Also, acquisition-oriented companies may require a *war chest* to guarantee themselves total flexibility and speed in making the big deal when it becomes available. Some companies even feel that interest rates may rise significantly so as to build liquidity for long-term needs; and while this may violate the anti-speculation philosophy of Chapter 12, it does not represent any fundamental conflict with a minimum-cash-and-capital philosophy. Finally, divestitures and some other revenue-generating projects can come up as a surprise, which results in temporarily high "excess" cash and capital balances until a new strategy for reinvestment can be developed. The increased usage of one such strategy, however, is perhaps the best evidence of the strength and growing acceptance of minimum cash and capital as the proper norm.

Cash buildups and utilization of excess debt capacity that do exist continue to be used more and more for stock repurchases (see Chapter 23) when other investment opportunities are inadequate. This had been an anathema to many corporate management teams in the past, but not nearly as much today.

Summary and Conclusions

The definition of capital has a significant effect in measuring the utilization and efficiency of business investment. Capital should be defined as interest-bearing funds plus shareholders' equity. Also, capital should be based on market value and not the book value. The cost of capital should be the weighted average cost of all sources of this interest-bearing debt and equity at their market values. Otherwise, the measurement of the returns on capital investment will not be useful.

Capital should be managed to increase the value of the firm. That is, either to minimize cost or to maximize the return or both. In other words, we should attempt to minimize interest-bearing liabilities and equity by minimizing fixed asset and current asset needs and by maximizing the interest-free liabilities within prudent limits.

CHAPTER 3

Buzzwords versus Financial Analysis: The Defense Never Rests

There are many times when some qualitative concepts are used to support business investments when the numbers are inadequate and the project unworthy. They may also constitute a device for raising some legitimate concepts that warrant consideration, even if the qualitative assessment does not offset all of the opposing bad news—such as the minor problems of a two percent return or a negative variable profit margin. After all, there are still naive analysts who feel two percent is an inadequate return. There are also people who use buzzwords in pretty-packaged binders to sell projects that can cost a company and its shareholders a fortune in losses or shortfalls of returns.

The Problem with Buzzword Rationales

The latest buzzwords are often used to support the current political views within a company. *Strategic imperative, market-share gains, long-term cost advantage,* and, of course, *synergies and economies of scale* are some of the more popular ones. You may have seen examples of this if you've read pamphlets from some of the top consulting firms with titles like "Discounted Cash Flow is Dead," or something similar.

Say, for example, that you review a major capital expansion program, let's say a new production/distribution center in Colorado.

Your results find an expected *discounted-cash-flow* (DCF) return of two percent. You strongly oppose a go-ahead decision on that basis. You could suddenly find yourself to be considered one of those low-level, stodgy, old-fashioned financial types who will be unenlightened by the obvious modern, sophisticated strategies and factors that can be used to justify such a project. But they may be wrong!

Proper Use of Qualitative Business Factors

We are strong proponents of all sorts of qualitative factors being given heavy weight in most major capital decisions. Take synergies, for example; they can be the most important factor in making an acquisition really pay off. This is especially true if the acquired business and the buyer's business were already both well run and properly valued by the market. The business could then become much more valuable in the hands of the buyer.

Complimentary product lines could add greatly to the sales of each sales force, with no increase in headcount. This could also reduce costs of production and distribution significantly as a result of consolidating some production and distribution facilities. The major caveat, however, is to require a demonstration of each synergy via its specific incorporation in a detailed set of pro forma financial statements and projections, based upon a detailed operating plan for the combined businesses. Without the numbers and assumptions to scrutinize, the synergies that sound logical may or may not be obtainable in practice.

Other qualitative factors similarly warrant consideration; but they should also be incorporated in the projected numbers wherever possible, and they should not be double counted. For example, once market-share and cost-saving factors are reflected in the projected results, and the DCF return is still only two percent, can strategic market-share and cost-structure factors be used to justify the project? Only if there is something left over and above the projections, that cannot be quantified, should the project be so defended.

Take an example in the chemical industry. In discussing capital expenditures procedures and hurdle rates, suppose we encounter purported practices of Dow, the prodigious market leader of the time. Suppose it is argued that Dow never really required 12 percent returns, and some of their best projects had projected returns well below that level. Of course, one could present a counter argument by saying that the actual results likely achieved 20 percent returns. In other words, ultra-liberal approaches and ultra-conservative projections may offset each other.

More importantly and more likely, there may be some major qualitative factors that can cause the actual returns to be high. Some strategic factors may exist, including market share or cost advantages, that were not projected, but are real. Of course, they may be mere windfalls. Possibly, Dow was merely lucky. Yet, there could have been known factors upon which the investment decisions were actually based by the company's senior management. Perhaps they were included in the real forecasted results that no one but the project sponsor ever saw. Perhaps they were not quantifiable at all on the front end, even if they were both known and really generated higher profits in the long run.

In general, therefore, most qualitative factors and buzzwords that bear consideration are those that will impact a DCF return. The excuse to cite them in support of an investment decision apart from the projected DCF return itself is that all or part of the benefits cannot be quantified on the front end. So, to avoid a financial mistake in this area, one should play the devil's advocate as a financial manager. Always ask two questions:

1. Are the touted benefits already incorporated in the projected results?
2. If not, why not?

You must always be aware, however, of the legitimate possibilities that some additional benefits can only be cited, not forecasted, on the front end.

Non-Business Factors to Consider

There is also a second type of qualitative factor that bears full consideration. Legal and ethical considerations are always legitimate points to raise in the decision process. While our goal is to maximize wealth for the shareholders by maximizing the value of the business assets and future cash-flow stream, there is no rule that we must commit illegal or unethical acts along the line.

On the other hand, it is not usually legitimate, but is a common blunder, to justify business investments based upon their charitable implications, apart from legitimate and ethical considerations. An exception would be if you are the sole owner of the business, so the money you are donating is your own. Another exception would be if there are likely marketing benefits or other business benefits from the good will that can be earned; but for the most part, charitable contributions are not part of business. When it's the shareholder's money you are playing with as a corporate manager, your favorite charity is not a proper consideration because the shareholder can decide, on his own, to donate to his favorite charity once the business profits are earned and distributed. Only if there is a likely business benefit from the charity, or a possible backlash if your firm fails to contribute, would there be a legitimate justification for charitable expenditures. If this is possible, such points must at least be raised.

Incorporating Risk

There may be a third type of qualitative factor, and in any case there is a third type of financial mistake in this area. *Risk* is often the key element in many of the qualitative factors cited to justify capital spending. When an industry is characterized as volatile, cyclical, or sensitive to an oil shortage, this is a combination of strategic planning and risk assessment. For risk factors, it is best to quantify the effects as much as possible, but we must also recognize that the final incorporation of risk into the decision process will probably be qualitative.

Risk is really the downside potential of a business. In forecasting, you should always project more than one scenario, and the forecasts for the likely worst cases represent the downside sensitivity analysis or risk. If the combination of the magnitude of the losses and the likelihood that the worst case scenario could occur are great enough, then the risk may force you to require a much higher return to be projected in your expected base-case scenario. In any event, the numbers for all the likely cases represent information to be included in the decision maker's thought process as representative of the upside potential and the downside risk.

Yet, there are two common misuses of this approach. First, redundancy runs rampant. Downside volatility is often cited as a strategic problem; on top of that, risk is cited as an added negative. Projections are reduced for the risks related to key revenue and cost assumptions, and then risk is heaped on as an added justification burden. While the name given to these types of decision inputs is not critical, separating them and avoiding double counting is obviously necessary to have a chance for an intelligent decision.

Second, the desire for a simple, routine answer will inevitably lead you to express the probabilities of all likely outcomes. To some optimistic people, a likely downside represents one chance in a hundred. To the pessimist, any identified downside can easily have a 40 percent chance of occurrence. This is called *probabilistic analysis*.

To demonstrate this problem, let us cite some personal experience in this use of probabilistic analysis in practice. In a major group of one sophisticated Fortune-200 corporation, a probabilistic budget was developed for each of the divisions and the overall group. The model utilized raw data assumptions and mathematical algorithms to develop revenue levels by category and expense levels by account. Since it was computerized, we ran 100 simulations utilizing a random number generator which converted the low point, projection, and high point for each assumption into 10 percent, 80 percent, and 10 percent probabilities.

The desired result was a 65 to 75 percent chance of attaining the budgeted profit levels. Then, with all subjective inputs having been input, low and behold, the output for each division was in the 65 to 75 percent probability range!

In the chemical industry, where research, technology, and long lead times create massive uncertainties about the future, we considered using probabilities for capital expenditure analysis. Yet, the experience of people in the field was similar. Either you could not properly prepare the probabilistic estimates or once you learned how to do it, the estimates always led to a calculated expected-value return similar to your original one-point projected return. Therefore, we did not include probabilities in our requirements, but merely a discussion of downside scenarios and the resultant lower returns.

Another means of quantifying risks when a business is new and most projections are very uncertain is called *break-even analysis*. You can back into a decision by determining what revenue and cost assumptions are required to achieve a required return; then, merely evaluate the reasonableness of these assumptions. For example, if we need to sell one million units to break-even, and if we feel we can sell two to ten million units, while uncertainty and volatility are still tremendous, our chances of achieving a good return appear to be excellent.

Inadequacy of Growth Target Rates

Now let's move to an entirely different area from risk, back to the fundamental issue of what level of returns should be required for a business at its average risk level. We emphasize cost of capital as the benchmark. Yet, higher or lower desired cutoff levels have been defended by some consultants for their CEO clients based upon growth targets. This concept was, in fact, almost always used as the basis of the capital expenditure evaluation system proposed by the corporate staff of one major company in the chemical industry. The approach did not hold up, however, when the internal financial and operating staffs asked some basic questions.

Mathematically, it is not difficult to calculate the returns required from investments to attain given growth targets. Basically, the required return must be equal to the growth target. If dividends are paid, then they must be funded by debt and the required return must be defined as a post-interest return. The following example should help demonstrate this point:

Original investment $= \$100$
Return $= 10\%$
Year 1 profits $= 10\% \times \$100 = \$10$
Dividends $= \$4$
Debt $= \$4$
Retained earnings $= \$6$
New investment $=$ Original $+$ Retained earnings $+$ Debt
$\qquad\qquad\quad\ = \$100 + \$6 + \$4$
$\qquad\qquad\quad\ = \$110$
Year 2 profits $= 10\% \times \$110 = \$11$
Growth rate $= (\$11 - \$10)/\$10 = 10\%$

But what if the growth target is 50 percent and the returns available on the full amount of investments are only 15 percent? Do we just make no investments and pay out all the assets in the form of dividends and repurchase of stock? Are we really saying that if we cannot grow at 50 percent, we do not want to grow at all? Well, of course, that cannot be the answer! Our chemical industry operating people knew that was a problem, and we financial types could not answer their queries based upon growth-target investment hurdle rates.

On the other hand, what if our growth target is only five percent and returns on investment available are a full ten percent? Do we have it made? Not if our shareholders require a higher return to satisfy them and to sell our stock would reduce the value of the company, then there could be a minor problem—like survival of the company!

So how low can you go in accepting returns on investment and growth targets? Well, you merely ignore growth targets (they will be a result of the return level and other factors), and concentrate on a return adequate to increase, or at least preserve, the value of the firm. Such a return level is called *cost of capital*.

Economies of Scale

One final point about buzzwords—the term *economies of scale* could be defined as the acquisition, development, or expansion of a business with low returns, but with enough saved on spreading all that "fixed" overhead to make up the difference. Yet, back in the food-service industry, we learned that in some cases, going from one unit to two units could mean diseconomies of scale. You need managers for each one to be on site, and you develope a need for senior management and accounting/information systems to control the unit managers.

Diseconomies do not result in every case, and if the units are relatively homogeneous, contiguous, and so on, there should be some definite savings by growing. Yet, you must review each situation carefully on a case-by-case basis.

In an acquisition, you must be especially careful when a large company acquires a small entrepreneur. While many economies of scale, synergies, and benefits of enlightened, sophisticated management are real and are invariably projected, diseconomies of scale are also usually quite real and they are rarely included in the projected results.

At CBS, for example, enlightened management was demonstrated by focusing on diseconomies involved with the buttoned-down management style, reporting systems, compensation policies, and so on, as well as the more obvious synergies and opportunities to consolidate management and operating functions. In other words, ask the right questions— what are the *synergies, economies of scale,* and *diseconomies of scale* as related to the specific operating plan that we can develop on the front end?

Summary and Conclusions

Qualitative assessment should be implemented for supporting business investment decisions, especially when the quantitative factors fail to support the project. Qualitative factors deserve heavy weighting in most major capital decisions. Yet, they should be quantified and incorporated in the projected numbers wherever possible. Nevertheless, where this is not possible, some additional benefits can only be cited, not forecasted, on the front end.

Non-business qualitative factors, such as legal and ethical considerations, should also be considered in the decision-making process. Risk may also be treated as a qualitative factor in many decisions. Misuses of qualitative assessment, however, can lead to misleading conclusions and investment disasters.

Residual Values and Their Importance: The End Justifies the Means

Overlooked Residual Values

There is one defense for mediocre businesses that does deserve full incorporation into our thinking. Remember the asset values cited in Chapter 1, apart from the value of the ongoing earnings stream? Many business investments can turn out to be profitable even if they fail. Thus, when you are buying a business, or investing in new assets to support a business for purely operating, non-liquidation reasons, the salvage value or residual at the end of your projected cash flows must still be taken into account. In many cases, the depreciated value is used. Yet, this is totally inadequate if the accounting depreciation is a pure fiction.

Various Types of Assets

When was the last time you saw real-estate investments depreciate? Yes, it does happen sometimes—for example, in parts of Texas in recent years—but how about prime, fungible real estate (such as office buildings, retail outlets, and even factories without special, esoteric equipment)? Yet, the likely appreciation of such assets is still often ignored by financial analysts or put down as a wild projection merely being used to offset otherwise mediocre returns. Of course, bankers do not overlook such values, as we will see in Chapter 20.

Another type of friendly financier also places great emphasis on the outcome of residual values—the *lessor*. In fact, if we did not account for an appreciating asset that the lessor owned at the end of the lease, a buy/lease analysis for an office building a few years ago could have shown an implicit interest rate (pre-tax equivalent of the break-even internal rate of return) below the company's A-rating borrowing rate. Since the lessor had a high borrowing rate and a need to make a profit, this appeared somewhat unusual. Now, we refused to believe in the philanthropy of the lessor, but, we also refused to believe that such real estate would not appreciate. Even a modest appreciation, equivalent to a modest inflation, would produce the expected two percent (200-basis-point) spread over the borrowing rate.

Take a look at computer leasing, however, and you find even significantly higher implicit interest rates. For example, in the mid-1970s, a computer-whiz vice president of information systems for a trucking industry group compiled tons of information on reliability and life cycles for used mainframe computers. When the figures were inputted into a buy/lease analysis, the resultant implicit interest rate was about 25 percent. The reason for this was not necessarily the sheer greed of the lessor, but the risk of obsolescence and its potential impact on residual values of computer mainframes, which were rapidly changing with technology. The obsolescence risk was very high, unless you could resell the equipment. This is where the more efficient computer-leasing firms made their money. They made use of resales or releases to smaller firms satisfied with "last year's models."

Unfortunately, if their assumptions had been wrong, great losses could have occurred. Computer leasing and leasing of other less fungible or recession-sensitive items (such as airplanes) became quite unprofitable for many companies as a result of this phenomenon. Yet, even some unusual big ticket assets can become fungible under certain operating game plans.

Moving more towards the heart of the trucking business, we had also found that the basic operations of two divisions relied greatly on manufacturers' financing. Company-owned truck fleets could be financed to a very high degree of leverage (meaning small down payment). Even owner-operators, with no significant net worth and modest annual income, could obtain financing of quite expensive truck tractors to haul the large trailers. While marketing support obviously played a part in the manufacturer's decision, he also knew that there was little risk involved due to the tangible nature of the asset and his resale expertise within the industry.

When a third division of the same group operated in the modular building field, there was a constant struggle with accountants and bankers about depreciation schedules and secured-financing values. It was known that individually leased units joined to construct a modular building could easily be separated and released in new configurations for new uses to a wide variety of different customers. The units were nearly as fungible as trucks, and truck leasing was done with heavy asset-based financing. Thus, the fundamental financial results—income statement effects of depreciation, debt-capacity, and returns on equity—were totally altered by the outlook for the residual values of assets.

Residual Value of Entire Businesses

Now let's move to an even bigger issue. What if the residual value is based on all the future earnings stream of an overall business, as opposed to specific assets? On the one hand, the residual value appears to be less important because, if the business fails, it could be difficult to liquidate it. On the other hand, if an acquisition of an entire business is being evaluated over a 10- to 15-year period, it is quite misleading to use a residual value based upon specific assets. If the business is successful and achieves the projected results, then in nearly all cases, the liquidation value of the ongoing business value should appreciate. Either the residual value will be high at the end of the projection period, or you probably have some more fundamental problems with your profit projections for earlier years.

The implications of not properly considering the residual value of an acquired or developed business are really quite grotesque. As individuals seeking relative safety and simplicity, we invest in such things as single-family homes. Yet, we do expect some increase in the market value, at least in current dollars, if not in present value or constant dollars. As corporate financial officers, however, seeking maximum profitability from our capabilities of taking risks and managing complex businesses, we invest in such businesses in their entirety. How can we then expect no appreciation in the resale value?

There are also those laymen who feel residual values do not matter if you use a long project life for your present value calculations. Experience shows that 10 to 20 percent of the present value is attributable to residual values even after 15 years, and more than 50 percent is likely if only a five-year life is used. Well, that's significant enough for any business.

Estimating Future Values

Now that we all agree on their importance, there are several ways to estimate future values of entire businesses, as opposed to merely the underlying assets. They can be as conservative and simple as you desire:

Inflated original purchase price. This assumes that any business projected to do well enough to justify an acquisition should at least retain its value.

Inflated original purchase price, plus capital spending, less cumulative depreciation. This assumes that the investment will merely yield a minimum required return within the firm to retain value and that depreciation represents the real decline in value with the passing of time.

Original purchase price/earnings ratio times last projected year's earnings. This assumes that the P/E ratio should at least be retained if the acquisition works out as planned; but this can be a problem because of all the factors, including many exogenous ones, affecting P/E levels.

Increased P/E times last year's projected earnings. This assumes that a good acquisition will always increase the P/E level, which is obviously a vulnerable assumption.

Capital gains taxes. This should be subtracted from all of the above methods.

We have even used a more conservative method in practice for the residual value in the financial projections. It is merely the initial purchase price of an acquisition or the cumulative cash investment of an internally developed business. This is obviously quite conservative because after our 15-year project lives, the initial costs understate replacement costs by at least 50 percent. These are values of businesses and not of plants and equipment that grow old or obsolete even if the businesses are healthy. Aside from being conservative, we are also eliminating manipulation; that is one of the greatest problems in this area. It would be easy for operating managers to save a marginal pet project without creating target results that would be difficult for them to achieve by merely increasing the resale price multiple—let's say from 10 to 12 times. Our method removes such manipulation because the only determining factor of the residual value is what you are already projecting as investment outflow in earlier years.

As you may have guessed, we might prefer an even more aggressive method for higher residual values. Yet, something is better than nothing. There are all sorts of conservative corporate "nay-sayers" who feel that any residual value is an attempt to justify a bad project. Unfortunately for them one still has to go out and negotiate against competitive bidders, who do know that most businesses do not fall over the cliff after a 10- to 15-year projection period. Lo and behold, they always seem to have an extra 10 to 20 percent to play with.

Newsworthy Assets for Credit and Buyout Decisions

Apart from overall businesses, real estate, and computers, what are some of the most critical values to forecast? Let's list a few that are often much more valuable than their low or non-existent balance sheet book values:

- Oil reserves
- Film libraries
- Brand names
- Subscriber lists
- Purchasing and employment contracts
- Broadcast licenses

For creditors, we feel these are all quite significant and do support the high-debt leverage potential discussed in Chapter 20. They are also significant additions to value, apart from the ongoing business, for equity investors and managers, as discussed in Chapter 10. It would be difficult to continue to run a business, though, without some of them—such as, the *Coca-Cola* brand name or a subscriber list. Yet, even these assets could be sold and leased back or licensed back (one exception might be a broadcast license).

With respect to leveraged buyouts, unfriendly acquisition takeovers, and corporate restructures (discussed in Chapters 20 and 23), these asset values are becoming increasingly noted and important. Again, basic finance should have focused more attention on the residual asset values all along. A knowledge of such basics can place them in a proper perspective today.

Summary and Conclusions

Do not ignore residual values. Proper calculation of residual values can critically influence an investment decision, sometimes with a surprisingly large impact. Buildings, machinery, oil reserves, subscriber lists, and a large number of other assets have residual values that must be incorporated in many investment or buy/lease decisions.

What Are the Relevant Variable Costs for Different Decisions?

Varying the Variables

Definitions of Key Terms

As you might guess from the above heading, semantics plays more than a passing role in the subject of this chapter. We will show how the definition of *variable cost* must vary with the purpose and circumstances, no pun intended.

Conceptually, what does variable or incremental mean? The words themselves have quite similar definitions in English. *Variable* means something that varies or changes. *Incremental* means something is added or subtracted.

The variability or incremental effect may be contingent upon a general change of circumstances or a specific causal factor. When the causal factor is the magnitude of the operating volume within the same organization/investment structure, and under the same operating strategies, then the changes represent *variability*. When the causal factor is a change in the organization/investment structure or in the operating strategies, then the changes represent *incremental effects*.

More specifically, with respect to cost changes, variability refers to costs that change as sales dollars, sale units, or production units change—hence the accounting term and account classification denoted as *variable costs*. Similarly, incremental effects refer to costs, as well as revenues, of one decision or set of circumstances versus another—hence the term denoted as *incremental costs*.

When we switch to an analysis of the bottom line (profits and not merely costs), accounting reports prepared under a *direct-cost* system automatically incorporate the effects of variability. All costs that vary with sales or production levels (variable costs) are expressed on a per-unit or a percentage of sales-dollar basis. As sales or production volumes change, they change. In fact, they are treated as inventory values, which are merely the capitalized costs of inventory, until they are sold. Costs that do not vary with sales or production levels are classified as *fixed costs*. They are treated separately in the analysis and are held constant within a range (for instance, fixed costs are fixed if you do not need an additional plant to manufacture a given level of production volume).

Be wary, however, to identify the accounting system that is employed by a given company. Most are *full-cost* systems, so fixed costs are also added to the per-unit costs or the per-sales-dollar percentages. If we are concerned with the effects of sales/production volume on costs and profits, we must first subtract all the fixed costs from the full-cost product cost to isolate the variable costs.

Once we have isolated the variable costs under either a direct-cost or full-cost system, then we can calculate variable profit from a given level of sales or production by merely subtracting those costs from the revenues. We can calculate total revenues and total costs separately for that level of sales or production; or, we can express revenues and costs on a per-unit basis or a percentage of sales-dollars basis, net them to obtain a variable profit per unit or a profit percentage of sales dollars, and then multiply that variable profit figure times the appropriate sales or production level.

Volume Variance Analysis

Before we continue, we should correct a secondary mistake often expressed by cost accountants, especially those with manufacturing plant experience, and even more especially where the plants are treated as cost centers not profit centers. This often poses a common ''can't see the forest for the trees syndrome.'' If you ask them what are the profit effects of a change in volume compared with budget expectations, they'll pull out their detailed full-cost accounting reports, and give you the volume variance figure. Well, what's wrong with that is that it is only one piece of a two-piece puzzle.

Volume variance is merely the effect on per-unit costs of spreading fixed costs over a smaller number of units under a full-cost accounting system. (This is the paradox learned by all accounting students—fixed costs "vary" per unit and variable costs are "fixed" per unit in the short term.) Since the spreading of such fixed costs, or the lack of variability of such fixed costs, is a part of the variable profit, the volume variances are obviously part of the answer. Yet, there is another part to the answer—namely the revenues over and above all costs per unit times the proper volume level, which is called full-cost profit. The two pieces together will equal variable profit as defined above.

Let's take a look at some sample calculations:

	Budget	Actual	Variance
Data inputs			
Units	100	110	10
Revenues	$1,000	$1,100	$ 100
Variable costs per unit	5	5	0
Variable costs	500	550	50
Fixed costs	300	300	0
Fixed cost per unit	3	2.73	0.27
Profit A	200	250	$ 50
Variable profit (Direct basis)			
Per unit	$ 5	$ 5	$ 0
Total A	500	550	$ 50
Volume variances (From full-cost accounting system)			
Per unit	$ N.A.	$ N.A.	$0.27
Total B	N.A.	N.A.	$ 30
Profit on additional volume (Full-cost basis)			
Per-unit profit	$ 2	$ 2	$ 0
Additional units	100	110	10
Profit C	$ 200	$ 220	$ 20

That is, the variable profit equals the full-cost profit on the additional units plus the volume variance, or:

$$A = C + B = \$20 + \$30 = \$50$$

For senior management decisions and for evaluation of line-management's cost control, it is critical to remove the entire effect of volume variances on profits. In practice, for a major non-manufacturing service group, the executive co-author developed a percent-of-sales variance analysis system to monitor the full effects on volume changes, even though the retail unit volumes and costs were unknown. The entire outlook of the adequacy of our cost control was modified so we could objectively concentrate on improvement in operations or marketing as necessary.

Incremental Cost Analysis

In doing an incremental analysis between two alternatives, we must do more than isolate the variable costs. We must also identify the fixed costs that will vary and the variable costs that will be fixed between two alternative decisions or sets of circumstances. For example, let's look at a new plant that is required to provide both volume and efficiency. The fixed costs associated with the manufacturing plants (such as depreciation, maintenance, some utility charges, and so on) will increase with the addition of a second facility. Yet, the new plant may eliminate certain labor-intensive operations so that a portion of the variable costs will not increase.

Finally, we must also identify any additional costs that are not shown in the existing accounting system. Our new plant may require some different manufacturing steps, pollution control procedures, and the like. These will certainly entail incremental costs, but they may be fixed or variable, depending upon the nature of required change. There is a similar problem we must address when the incremental analysis is aimed at a present value calculation for the final result.

Present values are based upon cash flows and not merely income. We must separate all the incremental costs, both fixed and variable, into cash and non-cash items. We must also identify non-income-statement cash items (such as new capital investments) and include them in our incremental cash flows.

Now, in practice, all this can be done relatively simply. If we concentrate on full income statements and cash-flow statements for each alternative, then these will provide a safety check for the inclusion/exclusion of all fixed and variable costs and all cash and non-cash costs, as relevant as required. Yet, you must still always ask whether or not and when a cash flow is required. For some items, the answer is merely an issue of timing. In the short run, costs can be fixed or non-cash. In the long run, many fixed costs vary and require new cash outlays. For example, added volume to support a geographical expansion may be within the production capacity of existing facilities. Yet, in the long run, the capacity will be used up sooner, so added fixed costs and cash outlays will be required at an earlier date. This effect should show up in a properly constructed set of incremental projections for future years.

Transfer Pricing

Let's take a look at another tangential mistake before we sum up. *Transfer pricing* is one of the more misunderstood concepts of our time. The real problem is that most businessmen seek a "correct" answer for the best transfer-pricing mechanism. The real solution is to start out with the understanding that all transfer-pricing mechanisms are "wrong," and that we should seek one that is the least wrong and/or one that yields the most favorable managerial/analytical results.

Transfer pricing attempts to duplicate results of independent businesses, even though they are all part of the same corporate entity. Yet, once you put two businesses under "one roof," there is no true measure of individual results. There are economies of scale and all sorts of other effects on the sales methods and cost structures. These distortions increase to the extent sales between the two businesses, known as *intercompany sales*, are significant, which is especially true of vertically integrated companies. Some examples would be production and sales divisions of a major retail chain or the engine production and car assembly divisions of an automobile manufacturer.

On the one hand, the producer of intermediate manufacture materials for another division in the same company may save a great deal of sales effort and cost, and may even have no problems with competitive bids. On the other hand, should the producer be allowed to earn a "normal" profit for such an advantageous setup?

There are two common approaches most companies use. The first treats the producer as a cost center and transfers all products internally at their cost—excluding profit, and with or without division overhead allocated to the full-cost product costs. The second treats the businesses as independent and transfers all products internally at the external fair market value. The latter may require negotiation and a presidential decree to resolve disputes, but a determination of a mutually acceptable market value is usually possible. Yet, which of these two methods is correct? The answer is neither or both, depending upon your personality. (Does the proverbial picture of the man in the middle of a rope show him climbing up or sliding down?)

If we merely recognize that no one right answer exists, and simply seek the "best" answer in terms of our management incentive goals, then we can use an approach used for a diversified, highly integrated chemical company in the second half of the 1970s. We listed the criteria that would support the *cost-center* and *market-price approaches*, respectively: for example, the percentage of products sold internally versus externally, the existence of market-price quotations, the strategic purpose for being in the intermediate-product business, and so on. We then determined which system represented the least of the evils. If a cost-center approach were used, we also transferred a share of the manufacturing investment on the balance sheet to calculate more representative return-on-investment ratios, since the profits of the buyer had already been aided by reduced costs from transfer prices without profits.

In terms of the main theme of this chapter, however, should the seller's fixed, as well as variable, costs be included? Of course, they should, if the intercompany sales and transfer pricing are part of a long-term strategy. Remember one paradox—fixed costs become variable in the long run, as new facilities are requested. If, however, these intercompany sales were specially arranged merely to pick up the shortfall from an industry recession, variable costs may be more representative.

Yet, the most important error in the transfer-pricing game is the failure to adjust the calculations for the incremental effect on the overall corporation. In deciding on production and sales volume levels, pricing, and the like, we must be sure someone up there (the corporate staff) is analyzing the consolidated effects on the corporation. There are production and marketing costs in *both* divisions and there is only *one* revenue stream from external customers. Also, incremental costs are the only costs relevant for decisions—as opposed to bookkeeping—they should be fixed, variable, or both, as discussed above, depending upon the alternatives being analyzed.

Summary and Conclusions

The purpose of this chapter was to eliminate confusion in handling incremental costs and to properly utilize fixed/variable cost classifications from the various accounting systems, especially for investment-decision calculations. (It was not to hassle you with financial semantics and paradoxes.) After all, how can you allocate resources among investment alternatives if you do not know the incremental costs, and thus profits, derived from each one. Apart from the special caveats with respect to accounting cost systems, volume variances, and transfer-pricing approaches, we can sum up the overall approach to use in practice as follows:

- Prepare a full income statement for each alternative
- Utilize the existing accounting system for classification of variable versus overhead costs (for example, direct-cost or full-cost systems)
- Define the incremental income statement as the difference between each alternative
- Modify the increment income statement:
  —Identify variable costs that do not change with specific incremental volume
  —Identify variable costs that change on a per-unit basis, so that the total changes in these costs are associated with a different alternative, as well as with a change in volume

—Identify fixed costs that change with the change in alternatives

—Identify fixed costs that change over the time frame of the projections

- Develop a cash-flow statement to tie in with the incremental income statement:

  —Remove non-cash items such as depreciation (really add back post-tax to leave the effect of a tax shield in place)

  —Add non-income cash items, such as required investment in fixed assets and working capital, both initially and over the time frame of the projections.

CHAPTER 6

The Creation of Value by Modifying Financial Documents

Statement of the Problem

If someone gives you 110 Canadian dollars in exchange for 100 U.S. dollars, have they added $10 to your net worth? We feel safe in saying the majority of you would realize the answer is contingent upon the exchange rate that exists between the two countries at the time in question. At a rate of C$1.10/US$ or more, the answer is obviously no. So how about an increase in the number of shares of stock in a given company, such as 200 new shares for 100 old ones?

Well, if you are the only one picking up some additional shares, then you are a winner. But if everyone receives more shares in the same company, has your ownership changed? No, only some paper has been shuffled about. And if your ownership is the same, has there been any increase in the value of the overall company? Not unless there are some inefficiencies in the marketplace, because an efficient market will have already accounted for the value of the company and ownership percentages.

Corporate Stock Transactions

Thus, a stock split—such as two new shares for each old share—gives the shareholder nothing, at least in terms of fundamental value. The benefits are, therefore, limited to two types other than the fundamental value. First, a stock split could serve as a communication device, since it often accompanies a rapid increase in stock prices. Yet, it should be argued that the same effect could be obtained if the investor relations department announced continued growth for the company and was believed by its investors. Second, optimal share prices may be under $100, supposedly so that round lots can be purchased by more investors. In addition, a stock split can be used to prevent the per-share price from increasing beyond that level.

While stock splits are no longer the area for many financial mistakes, stock dividends are still proposed by many as an acceptable alternative to cash dividends when the company needs to retain earnings for investment requirements. We will discuss dividend policy in Chapter 24. Yet, a stock dividend that merely gives every shareholder more shares of stock has the same effect as a stock split. While there may be benefits from retaining the cash within the company, and there may be benefits from telling everyone what you are doing, it does not seem to be any different from merely announcing your intentions and following one of the acceptable cash dividend programs discussed in Chapter 24. As we will see, these programs include the lowering of the dividend if an internal need for funds changes. The only benefit may be the reduced per-share price level, as discussed above, but that is rarely the one cited as one of the main reasons for stock dividends.

Stock dividends have also been cited as tangible measures of the wealth being retained on behalf of the shareholder in the company. Well, that is no more true, if you give all shareholders some more shares via a stock dividend, than foregoing all dividends. The only tangible element is the communication.

It has also been suggested that the stock dividend can be sold in the market in order to give shareholders wanting cash the same amount as a cash dividend would offer. This would still leave the value of the remaining shares as high as before, since retained earnings increased the overall value of the company. Yet, if no stock dividend were ever used, and the retained earnings increased the value of the company, the shareholder would still be able to sell a portion of his shares to attain the exact same effect. This is assuming that public relations announcements on the use of the retained earnings were made to increase the value of the overall company.

Now, what if you are not given shares of stock, but an opportunity to buy them at a discount price? Again, this subscription offering is often treated as a separate type of financial strategy. An increase in the value for the overall company, maintenance of share prices, and a bargain for the existing shareholders who obtain rights to purchase additional shares at significant discounts may all be assumed as benefits. In reality, however, this is merely another form of a stock split; and the overall value of the existing shares cannot increase merely as a result of all shareholders receiving warrants.

Let's take a look at some calculations to demonstrate this point:

- Data inputs:
  —Existing price of stock = $10
  —Subscription discount price = $5
  —Existing number of shares = 100
  —Subscription shares = 100
- New value of company:
  —Original value = $1,000
  —New proceeds = $500
  —New value = $1,500
- Per-share prices:
  —Original price = *$10*
  —New price = $7.50
  —Subscription price = $5
  —Value of rights = $2.50
- Value per original share:
  —1 share @ new price = *$7.50*
  —1 right = $2.50
  —Total = *$10*

Thus, the overall value of the company should increase only by the amount of the proceeds. The value of the combination of existing shares plus rights should hold at the original price per share of $10. The per-share price, itself, should fall to $7.50, unless the communication element or the lower optimal per-share price-range concept have an impact. These two benefits may certainly exist, but would work exactly the same as discussed above for stock splits.

Another benefit has been raised for stock rights and subscription offerings, which is similar to the fallacious cash argument used to support stock dividends that we discussed above. In this case, the cash benefit is derived from the stock sale proceeds received rather than the earnings retained. Again, while this may be a benefit if the funds can be invested at high enough profit returns, that element is independent of the discount-price rights offering.

The investment of any proceeds at higher than the cost of capital will increase the overall value of the firm over and above the proceeds themselves. This is true for any stock offering, just as it is true for any retained-earnings decision in lieu of a cash dividend. Subscription discount offerings and stock dividends, however, add nothing new to this concept, except the possible benefits of investor-relations communication and a reduction in per-share prices to a lower optimal level. To reiterate, we feel the communication aspect can be handled in many other ways, and the per-share price concept should be addressed separately, even if one of these mechanisms—stock split, stock dividend, or stock rights discount offering—is chosen to accomplish the reduction.

Equity-Related Debt Issues

A fourth area of paper shuffling presents an analogous, but different attack on the efficient market hypothesis. Indeed, it is an attack on any concept of fundamental financial valuation. Convertible-debt securities convert into common stock at a fixed ratio. Debt securities with attached warrants allow purchase at a fixed price. As shown in Chapter 18, the purpose for the issue was to obtain new equity at an ultimately cheaper cost in the future than a straight issue of stock at the present time. Also, during the debt period, a lower interest rate is obtainable as a result of the equity kicker. Yet, do the risks of non-conversion, as well as the discount rate used to calculate present value for the equity proceeds, offset these benefits?

Let's also see what is happening on behalf of the investor. He is getting a chance for equity gains, but with no more apparent risk than any debt creditor. So, is this a case where both the issuer and the investor get a good deal as a result of some paper shuffling?

When compared with straight debt or stock issues, this may very well be the case. The issuer's benefits of lower costs of debt and/or equity can be considered similar to insurance premium profits over and above expected insurance losses in return for providing an insurance service to the investors. The latter needs an insurance policy to allow them to participate in the risky equity markets without higher risks.

Yet, are there no other "insurance policies?" Can the investor not simulate the same effect by utilizing separate segments of the capital markets? Can he not invest a slightly lower amount in interest-income securities, and then invest the remaining funds in a stock call option, to provide the equity upside kicker? The answer is probably yes, where the options market exists for a given stock. Yet, it may be easier to construct an insurance policy for most stocks via convertible debt and stock warrants. Also, the combined instrument, *convertible debt* or *debt with warrants*, provides convenience. And, after viewing prices of fancy frozen food entrees in the supermarket, we all know that the rewards for such convenience products are profits. Is a lower capital cost for the issuer than merely analogous to profit from insurance premiums?

Thus, there could very well be some good news for both the issuer of and the investor in convertible-debt and debt-with-warrant securities. This may be viewed as an arbitrage situation, where the equity and debt markets together are not functioning perfectly, but are allowing some advantages. Please note, *arbitrage* can be defined as the existence of a comparative advantage for an issuer in one of two markets, and his use of both markets in such a manner as to obtain a net savings from that advantage. Even if this is a case of arbitrage, however, it is not necessarily inconsistent with the general efficient market hypothesis described in Chapter 12. After all, "efficient" does not mean "perfect."

This phenomenon may, therefore, also be viewed both as an insurance service and as an arbitrage opportunity. In fact, you could cite financial service businesses, in general, and insurance businesses, in particular, as examples of significant arbitrage opportunities allowing the investor/lender/insurer to obtain a package deal better than he can obtain for himself on a risk-adjusted return basis.

Summary and Conclusions

Shareholders should keep in mind that an increase in the number of shares may not benefit you in terms of the overall value of your stocks. Generally, an increase in the number of shares has no direct benefit, but merely an announcement effect. In most cases, this effect also depends on the value of the company (such as the company's growth prospects). Therefore, increases in the number of shares alone cannot increase the overall value of the shares. (Yet, it may reduce the per-share price to a lower optimal level for round-lot trading.)

Another area of paper shuffling is convertible debt, which can be viewed as either an insurance service or as an arbitrage opportunity. It is considered a low-risk deal for equity-seeking investors, but this does not mean it is risk free.

CHAPTER 7

What Are the Relevant
Profit Returns to Consider?

Flexible Definitions
of Return on Investment (ROI)

The name of the game, or at least at the bottom line of the scorecard, is one's long-term return on investments. All of us in business know that is the goal for any well-run company, just as it is for any personal investment portfolio. But what exactly is the relevant investment to consider, and what is the exact return that should be employed?

For starters, we all know that the relevant return for an investment portfolio is the return on money you invest. And if your friendly broker or banker finances you, you need not count that as your investment, but merely reduce your profit return by the interest paid. Right? Well, if the portfolio consisted of Braniff Airlines stock before their crash, who takes a bath on the portion you borrowed? Unless you declare bankruptcy, you do.

So maybe you should require an adequate return on all of the invested funds whether they are borrowed or not. That is why individuals, as well as corporations, might want to consider returns on capital more relevant than returns on equity. And once you determine the optimal debt/capital ratio, as discussed in Chapter 20, then only the comparison of returns on capital with the optimal cost of capital is relevant.

For a corporation, there is also another way to reach the same conclusion. If you increase your return on equity by employing debt leverage above the optimal level, then your overall capital costs will increase, thereby increasing the discount rate for your profits, which reduces the value of your stock. Thus, this constraint on debt capacity may be more obvious for a corporation, though it exists for all investors.

Even if we all agree that return on total capital invested is the relevant measure, there are several ways to calculate that return using the same concept of capital discussed in Chapter 2. Each is relevant for a specific purpose. As seen in Chapters 1 and 4, the book value of assets may be significantly lower than their market values. Since we should define capital as either total assets less interest-free liabilities or total interest-bearing debt plus equity (see Chapter 2), we would greatly understate capital, as well as assets and equity, by using book value rather than market values. Yet, both are meaningful in determining the adequacy of returns, but for two different purposes.

Original Investment Decisions

If the goal is to evaluate the original investment decision, then dividing current profits by historical book values provides the more relevant measure of return on capital. If your goal is to evaluate the adequacy of the business against a potential divestiture opportunity, then the denominator should be the current market value of capital.

Similarly, if your goal is to evaluate the adequacy of business returns against the cost of funds, market values should be used on a weighted average basis. This is discussed in Chapter 2 and should coincide with the effect of leverage on capital costs in the revalued cost of capital, as discussed in Chapter 20.

Of course, present value calculations should be employed for the most accurate analysis of either case. Then the actual amounts and timing of the historical cash investments can be accounted for in evaluating the original investment decision. For the current divestiture decision, the market value of the proceeds, plus debt assumed by the buyer, less any capital gains taxes, can then be treated as an opportunity-cost investment outflow made to retain the cash flows from the business.

Broadcasting provides one of the best examples of this phenomenon. Television stations have escalated so dramatically in price that they have one of the highest returns on capital in CBS' consolidated reported results, but a mediocre return on likely market values. This retention could be based on the integral nature of the major metropolitan stations with the national television network we also own. This could very well be true for the other two networks, who also own their major metropolitan affiliate stations. There are two other possible rationales, of course—continued appreciation of the stations or a rapid growth in the future cash flows—but we personally emphasize the network explanation. In any case, this shows how radically a return calculation can and should be altered for different purposes.

An analogous situation arises when many non-tangible capital-intensive businesses are evaluated. Take another one of CBS' present businesses, magazines, where the most valuable assets are usually intangible—especially, the subscription list and good will. If the business is developed internally, then these assets are not reflected on the balance sheet. The investment is really the cumulative losses from the process of running the magazine until enough subscribers are obtained and enough advertising is generated to turn it into a profitable operation. If a profitable magazine is acquired, however, most of the purchase price will be reflected on the new balance sheet as the subscription list and good will. So what is the relevant return on capital?

Continuation/Divestiture Decisions

Well, if you are evaluating the feasibility of continuing in the business and making relatively minor investments in working capital or fixed assets required (see Chapter 2 as a reminder of the potential for low working capital in the magazine business), then the return on tangible capital is most relevant. Whether or not the magazine had ever been sold before, neither the value of subscription list nor good will need be reflected in the denominator to lower the return. Yet, if you are considering a divestiture of the business, then the market resale value is obviously the key. Return on total capital may be a proxy for this market value only if there had been a recent acquisition of this magazine to place the subscription list and good will on the balance sheet at values similar to those in the current market environment.

Again, for a real divestiture decision, utilize present values, cash flows, and market-value opportunity costs. Also, to evaluate the original internal-development decision, the present value of cash flows must be used in order to account for the investments in the major assets (the subscription list and good will) since they are merely the cumulative cash outflows from losses incurred in developing the business.

Inflation-Adjusted Returns

Now let's look back at the television station example. Remember the dramatic price escalation? Perhaps it could lead one to become a believer in utilizing inflation-adjusted financial statements usually required to be shown as supplemental information in annual reports. That information could certainly be useful. Yet, it can also certainly be quite misleading.

If the profit returns, based upon today's earnings and the inflation-adjusted investment, are low, that does not necessarily reflect the likelihood that further reinvestment or the failure to divest is unjustified. On the other hand, any investment is justified by future earnings levels, not merely by the current level, and future earnings of healthy businesses usually show growth. To evaluate continued investments or retention of a business, therefore, the potential for future growth must be protected. Nevertheless, inflation-adjusted returns are also not meaningful in evaluating past investment performance. The unadjusted inflation profits in the ROI numerator are relevant and represent growth to date that may have been and should have been forecasted when the investment was originally made in the past, at past cost levels. Yet, there is no reason to increase that investment to evaluate the real benefits or returns that it has already generated.

The main usage of inflation-adjusted returns, however, is as a red flag for investment, retention, and even new investment decisions. Once you have determined today's resale and/or replacement values, then an inflation-adjusted return will demonstrate how much profit growth must be attained to increase that return to an adequate level.

This is especially true in capital-intensive industries, such as the chemical industry. We have seen the return on replacement value assets used in the internal reporting systems emphasized at monthly management reviews. This approach assured that maintaining the fundamental profitability of the business in the long run (in terms of returns on assets) was always considered as an important goal.

Of course, future prices and profits are not included in such measures. Yet, these are the ones to be obtained over the future life of any reinvestment. Again, to be boring, redundant, and precise when the actual reinvestment decision, retention-versus-divestiture decision, or new investment decision is made, actual cash inflows and outflows must be projected to account fully for the time value of money, as well as future growth.

International Investments

When we leave the confines of our own nation, and its one economic system, determining relevancy becomes much more difficult. In terms of avoiding financial mistakes, this chapter, up until now, has been child's play, but the question of relevant returns for international investment becomes quite an adult problem.

What is relevant currency measured by? Which country's inflation rate should be used in projecting growth? Which tax rate is relevant? These are all difficult questions requiring answers. Even the general definition of investment, cash outflows, profits, and cash inflows requires very specific modification. Finally, as you might expect, the benchmarks for deciding on the adequacy of profit returns ultimately calculated must also be revised.

All of these concepts are discussed in Chapter 11 in connection with the evaluation of international capital expenditures. After reading it, you may see how each of the above questions are relevant and complex, but also answerable. With respect to this chapter, you may see their relevancy for calculating profit returns of existing investments, as well as those of new investments.

Relations of Buyer and Seller Returns

Earlier, we cited the opportunity-cost-investment approach to calculate the proper returns for any decision on potential divestitures. The last of the financial mistakes we find common in this area involves this approach. On the one hand, there is the failure by the novice to see the relationship between the opportunity-cost return of the seller and the return expected by the buyer. Basically, they are the same, if we exclude taxes and any synergies of the business with the buyer's or seller's other operations. On the other hand, of course, is the failure of the experts to note the tremendous effect that the seller's capital gains taxes, other differences in tax rates, and the many potential synergies can have on the return calculations. The same discussion in Chapter 1 on synergies and the post-acquisition stock-price multiples is just as relevant for this purpose. Without the synergies and tax differences, a good deal for the seller—in terms of both a high purchase premium and an inadequate opportunity-cost return—would mean a bad deal for the buyer. With the synergies and tax differences, a good deal for the seller could still mean a good deal for the buyer or an even worse deal than that alluded to above.

Of course, from a practical standpoint, all acquisition/divestiture professionals should address the other guy's reasons for a deal. This will obviously help them to be more effective in negotiations. Even more important, however, this will also aid them in being sure that they have properly analyzed all the aspects of the deal from their own perspective. We could cite several specific examples where returns for buyers limited the prices that could be paid for businesses. Yet, the return lost on the net proceeds by the seller could then be quite high. The buyer, therefore, would require either synergies with his own business (a more optimistic outlook for the business than the seller had), or a different set of long-term goals, to justify such prices.

Sometimes, if leveraged buyouts by management are involved, they are willing to take risks of increasing or retaining high-profitability levels that would make returns on their investments adequate. Also, any diseconomies of scale or the inefficiencies that they could see could be removed easily after such an acquisition. Finally, the leverage itself lowers the capital costs and the required return to allow their investment goals to be met, while the selling parent corporation's returns, lost by the sale, are still not high enough to force retention of the business.

Summary and Conclusions

The significant measure of business operation is the return of the investment. The determination of relevant methodology to calculate the return depends on its purpose. For example, book value balance sheet assets should be used to evaluate the original investment decision and the market value for current decisions. Nevertheless, both may not be very relevant when non-tangible capital-intensive businesses are evaluated. Similarly, inflation-adjusted returns should be used for reinvestment decisions, while unadjusted returns should be used for original investment decisions. Also, acquisition and divestiture returns for the buyer and seller, respectively, must account for the differences in synergies and tax treatment. Therefore, different return calculations should be made for different purposes.

CHAPTER 8

Macro Effects
of Takeover Phenomena

Effects on the Overall Economy

Since unfriendly acquisition takeovers have become America's most popular sport, it is difficult to resist discussing the topic. While there are allusions to takeovers and their relationship to asset values and debt leverage in several chapters, the increasing number of these phenomena in recent years makes it important to address this topic more directly.

While there are no easy answers to the question of whether corporate takeovers are good or bad for the economy, we do feel we can go back to the basics of finance and business to outline the issues and the pro and con factors. For starters, it is true that most companies may be worth more in parts than they are as a whole. This is true even for some of the largest companies, despite the benefits of economies of scales. It is also true of many of the most profitable companies, despite the favorable effects of profit performance on stock prices.

Economies of Scale and Strategies

First, perhaps we should look at size and the potential for increased value being created through economies of scale. As discussed in Chapter 3, economies of scale can be both created and eliminated for a given company through both acquisitions and divestitures.

If a large corporation is acquired by another large corporation, usually there should be significant savings potential from the consolidation of the corporate staffs. Additional economies of scale might be obtained if the operations of both companies could be organized within the existing groups and/or divisions of the buyer, thus eliminating some group or division overhead expense of the seller.

To the extent that the two companies are in different types of businesses and/or have different styles of management, reporting, and control, then the development of a new infrastructure to handle both sets of operations could easily involve diseconomies of scale. New group/ division organizations and cumbersome, duplicative reporting systems could be required. The transition period could be quite costly. Geographical moves are expensive. And most of all, management unfamiliar with the key elements of the new businesses under their control could reduce such operations to impotency.

As examples of the latter, the technology/cost emphasis of the chemical industry, the brand name advertising orientation of the soft drink industry, and the continual changing product in the broadcasting and record industries make the keys to successful management quite different for each of them. For chemicals, multi-billion-dollar commitments for five to ten years are often necessary. For soft drinks, rapidly changing advertising/promotion programs and expenditure levels are required to preserve market share. For broadcasting and records, each year represents a new ball game, with the current programming and record releases totally changing much of the business.

Nevertheless, economies of scale are often present with the combination of two companies, and the value of the two should increase. If the acquisition is then coupled with immediate divestitures of selected product lines to other companies where there is a good fit, the chances for economies of scale are even greater. The operation will ultimately wind up in a group or division organization where overhead can be eliminated and management may already be familiar with the product lines. When such cases result from either a ''good-fit'' merger of two large companies or the sale/resale of individual businesses, then that brings us to the magic word ''synergy,'' which raises even greater prospects for increases in value.

As discussed in Chapter 3, synergies can also be created and eliminated by both acquisitions and divestitures. If one or more of the product lines being sold winds up in a familiar home, then in addition to economies of scale and the absence of diseconomies of scale, several synergic benefits may be obtained. Vertical integration with suppliers and/or customers could be obtained, which would eliminate much of the marketing expenses required to or from the acquired business. Consolidation of operations in the same business allows each sales force to expand sales through product-line additions and/or allows reductions in the combined sales and marketing expenses. Production and other facilities can also be combined to generate savings, plus manufacturing overhead, technology, and patents can be shared, and so on.

Remember, however, the theme of Chapter 3. Economies of scale and synergies are popular buzzwords that are used as often to defend losing propositions as they are to describe real benefits. Quite frequently, consumer company diversification plans assume any product sold to the customer is right up their alley—high tech or low tech, advertised or not, brand name or commodity type, and so on. So you just can't raise the possibilities of synergies and economies of scale, but you must also play devil's advocate as to the reality of any savings.

If synergies and economies of scale are real, however, then their macro effect on the overall economy is to increase both value and efficiency. The benefits of Adam Smith's "invisible hand" in properly allocating resources to their most valuable uses would apply. Think about it. Economies of scale and synergies must allow corporate America to provide more goods and services to the customer at reduced prices.

Benefits of Proper Valuation

Now what if the economies of scale or synergies are unavailable, but a premium price to be paid for a company's businesses and/or assets is more than justified by its fundamental values. In other words, without the takeover phenomenon, is much of corporate America undervalued by the stock market, and do takeovers then help to eliminate this distortion? We guess to some extent it must be true. After all, not all acquisition prices are justified or based solely on synergies and economies of scale. If an undervalued stock market does explain at least some of the recent takeovers, then what are the macro effects on the overall economy?

Unlike the case with economies of scale and synergies, we cannot point directly to the savings that will result from the mere proper valuation of corporate assets and businesses. Yet, the net effect of the property-valued resources is good for society in the long run. We will leave it at that to avoid getting any more bogged down in the muck and mire of abstract economic philosophy.

Increased Debt Leverage

More important than undervaluation situations, the takeover phenomenon has had the effect of eliminating some of the suboptimal leverage problems. Both hostile takeovers and anti-takeover defenses employ leverage as a potent weapon. As discussed in Chapter 20, *leveraged buyouts* are often the form utilized by the takeover artist to buy and quickly resell a company in parts without using much of his own money.

In order to defend their shares, the target company, therefore, often adds enough debt to remove this leveraged-buyout capacity. To the extent the target company had been afraid to use the optimal amount of leverage (which is properly in the 50 percent range for many companies, as discussed in Chapter 20), the takeover artist winds up doing a favor for the target's management. Of course, there are risks of going too far; but until recently, probably many more major companies were underleveraged than overleveraged.

Now how about the overall economy? Is leverage good or bad for safety, or for growth? These are two main questions we have heard. First, we are increasing risks of bankruptcy on a scale that will undermine the whole economy. Yet, this assumes that leverage is already at the optimal level, and neither our understanding of it nor the stock market reactions appear to support that. While there is obviously added risk, it is the level of risk deemed desirable by the capital markets. Second, the debt capacity and total capital that are utilized for takeovers may not be available for new investments that are desirable. Then such investments will face a capital/debt-rationing problem. The basic principles of finance should give us quite a bit of comfort in this area.

The real constraint for new investment is the ability to generate a return over and above the cost of capital. To the extent leverage is increased to a level designated as optimal by the capital markets, then the overall cost of capital funds utilized by American industry will be reduced. Interest rates and the related debt cost will be increased because of the additional financial risk, even if it is prudent; the required return for shareholders will increase for the same reason. Yet, the weighted average is the cost of capital or the benchmark against which the new investments must be measured.

In other words, there is not some arbitrary capital rationing constraint (which every good finance major knows cannot be defended), but there is a basic question of required returns that determines the level of expenditures. If our analysis on the optimal degree of leverage and its effect on the cost of capital is correct, then takeovers that push the economy towards that leverage level aid long-term capital investment growth by reducing the required returns that must be earned.

There is one exception in our minds. That is the use of *junk bonds*, especially those given to the selling shareholders of the target companies. Call us naive, but we still feel bank credit analysis provides some safeguards. We are not sure this is true in the area of junk bonds. Do the selling shareholders properly discount a premium price offered for their shares when the bulk of the payment is a mere piece of paper with a promise to pay? The paper may be backed with no assets beyond those of the company being bought, and the new management of the company, charged with the responsibility of utilizing those assets, will be outsiders with no special experience or expertise.

The discount rate for such a risky transaction should be that of a risky equity investment, since a substantial increase in value of the business is necessary to pay off the paper. If such a discount rate of 40 to 50 percent pre-tax were used, the premium could easily disappear. Yet, it is common to think of 15 to 20 percent interest rates being adequate to discount such paper in many of the hostile takeovers reviewed in the press. It seems they are confusing a debt-form with an equity-risk reality.

Product-Line Pricing and Asset Liquidation

Another fundamental aspect of many turnovers is the resale of product lines. If a conglomerate is purchased and broken up as a result of the resales, then the effect may be the same as that which the corporation might have sought as part of their own corporate planning. Product-line pruning and unbundling of conglomerates became quite popular goals in the late 1970s and reversed the drive towards conglomerates of the early 1960s. Now, the macro effect is obviously to reduce diversification in companies themselves, and to leave diversification to that being provided by portfolios of securities from many different companies.

There is mixed empirical data as to the value of diversification within a company, apart from the security portfolio of many companies. There is also the risk of the management in one undiversified business becoming gun shy and not taking the types of prudent risks necessary to make the business progress and grow. Yet, if unbundling is a better idea for the overall economy than diversification of companies, then takeovers could provide some impetus for the net positive benefits.

Reduced Competition

A more commonly discussed and more economic criterion, as opposed to a financial one, is the concentration effects of takeovers. If large companies are bought by larger ones, or if the individual businesses wind up being bought by large companies, the large companies of today will be even larger tomorrow. Concentration from horizontal mergers can obviously be anti-competitive. Concentration from vertical mergers may also be anti-competitive in some situations. The progressive influence of the large companies, however, could represent both economic and political concentration apart from any specific business or product line. Thus, if the takeover phenomenon reduces the number of smaller, independent companies, there could be a fundamental change in the concentration of economic and political power within our society.

Corporate Employment and Careers

Another more sociological concept is the effect of takeovers on us poor working stiffs—whether we wear blue or white collars. Takeovers create uncertainty. Which company will be next? Will the takeovers result in the elimination of jobs or a total change in the working conditions and compensation expectations? Will anti-takeover defenses have similar effects? Can people no longer plan to devote their lives to hard work in a given company, industry, or functional area? Will the overall opportunities in a given industry or function be reduced by concentration? All of these questions may have affirmative answers that could have negative effects on the overall economy.

Even if the takeovers do not permanently scare away employees, there are also severe short-term effects on the economy. Unemployment can become high during transition periods of consolidation in specific industries or functional areas. Also, since the problem can arise suddenly and it requires a time-consuming structural change for a solution (such as retraining), the damage can be disproportionately great.

Yet, the problem does not appear to be great enough to affect the economy adversely as a whole in any noticeable manner. It is true that we can cite hundreds of cases where members of the middle and upper management groups have suffered permanent, significant damage, both to their careers and their net worth. The unemployment statistics, however, have shown strong improvement through the acquisition, liquidation, and leveraged-buyout booms of the 1980s. Also, the major problems we have seen in the midst of prosperity are in other types of economic pockets, such as the oil patch and the farm belt. If a major group of workers has been particularly vulnerable, then industrial laborers, as opposed to service laborers, win more of our concern than management groups.

Nevertheless, in the longer term, our economic capabilities are being drained. More of our brightest young managers and MBAs are going to the trading-of-wealth areas, such as Wall Street, and are no longer considering the professional management of major corporate resources to generate that wealth, which made America great, as a viable career path. They can earn much more money and suffer no greater risks than their corporate manager colleagues. Yet, where will our wealth come from in the future (especially in the increased global competition environment) without our own core of top-flight managers to counter the Japanese and others?

On the other side, countermeasures of excessive severance pay and golden parachutes may protect the employees, including executives. Yet, these also have high costs for the economy. Of course, the elimination of undervaluation of companies being taken over could generate more than enough value to cover such costs.

How about overall management capabilities? Some managers could be scared away into other professions. Yet, for specific takeover candidates, one must ask if it was the management's success or failure that was the cause for the company's vulnerability. For example, CBS became a target for takeover after achieving a record year in profits and being well positioned in its major businesses. The takeover threat has often been cited as a means of keeping management on their toes and trying their best. But we have seen many cases where management success suddenly makes a business a desirable takeover target.

If takeovers involve the elimination of poor management, that should be a help for the overall economy. Yet, the opposite situation is often true, and this could hurt the allocation of resources through discouragement of good management responsible for such allocation.

Summary and Conclusions

So where are we coming out? Well, unfortunately, not exactly in a crystal clear looking glass where all the right answers are easily seen. Instead, we are still walking around in a low-light swamp where you can sink in quicksand at any wrong turn and there are no signposts outlining the path to safety.

We do, however, have some oversimplified conclusions. Takeovers are probably good if they eliminate poor management, which is one of the worst dangers to the proper allocation of resources. Friendly takeovers are also probably good when they provide synergies and economies of scale, as long as they do not contravene the constraints of the anti-trust laws on illegal concentration. Our gut reaction is that takeovers are bad when they do not satisfy these criteria, despite the many other effects we have already discussed.

The real reason for the uncertainty as to the effect of takeovers is the separation of two elements in the U.S. economy that have been linked in simpler or older economies. *Management* and *ownership* are no longer the same in most cases. The economic benefits of optimally allocating resources may wind up hurting management, even though both the owners and the overall economy are benefited. The opposite may also be true for poor management that becomes more secure when business prospects are not so bright as a result of suboptimal resource allocation. It is difficult, therefore, to develop a system that gives the proper incentives to management and still maintains the best effects for the overall economy.

We feel the takeover phenomenon must be evaluated in this light as a very complex problem that may not be solved in the foreseeable future. For a given situation, however, some obviously correct answers may be identifiable. Also, asking some of the relevant, basic financial questions should, at least, shed some more light on this dark takeover swamp.

CHAPTER 9

Ranking Alternative Investments

Situations Requiring Ranking

Now, if we are all sure of what represents a good investment versus a bad one, what happens if we have two good opportunities? Can we take them both? Well, what if they are mutually exclusive—such as an East Coast plant versus a West Coast plant, with either one adequate to serve all of our national volume needs? Or what if there is only enough money in the capital budget to fund one project at this time—such as enough money to retool the automobile line and truck line, but not both? Obviously, we have now uncovered the need for a system to rank several good projects and choose the best for our needs.

Maximizing Total Value

You may have read many financial textbooks with their complicated, esoteric comparisons of the various ranking criteria—especially the *internal rate of return* (IRR) and the *net present value* (NPV). The approach taken is often highly mathematical, dealing with the problem of multiple roots and reinvestment rates implicit in the calculations. We feel we can understand the basic differences and benefits without resorting to such computations.

Suppose there are two great projects with a 100 percent return on each. Now, suppose they are either mutually exclusive or we can afford to fund only one of them. The first yields a 100 percent return on $1 million. The second yields a 20 percent return on $100 million. Since the projects are generally in the 10 to 20 percent range of returns, 100 percent is definitely great. But, which would you choose? You don't need to be a mathematical whiz kid to choose the bigger one, with the lower return, because it gives you more total value over and above your required return.

If you look at it carefully, that is all that the net present value calculation does. It shows the total value derived from a project over and above the amount necessary to cover the capital costs. The latter is accounted for by the discount rate used in the NPV calculation, which is usually labeled the *opportunity cost* or more precisely, the *cost of capital*. (See Chapter 16 for a more complete discussion of these related concepts.)

So, we have concluded that while a high return on a large project is obviously better than the same return on a smaller one, a high return on a smaller project may not be preferable to a merely good return on a large one. Then, how do we know where the combination of a size and return is optimal? Why, we just select the highest net present value.

Percentage Returns versus Present Values

The next point is that the only difference between the internal rate of return and net present value criteria appears when you are ranking two projects. In terms of projects selection, they *always* yield the same answer. If the net present value is positive, using a given discount rate, then the internal rate of return *must* exceed that discount rate. If the NPV is negative, then the IRR *must* be less than the discount rate. If the NPV is zero, then the IRR *must* equal the discount rate.

So for capital project evaluations, if you prefer to use a relative measure (like the internal rate of return), rather than an absolute measure (like the net present value), go right ahead and do so. We find most executives prefer to use a relative measure. One gets a sense of magnitude by comparing 100 percent, 15 percent, 30 percent, and so on. But what message does $150,000 net present value convey? Why, nothing, until we know the magnitude of the accumulative investments, or better yet, the internal rate of return.

Even for ranking two projects, we can still use an internal rate of return and always obtain the same precision of automatically accounting for the different magnitudes of different projects that we just discussed for the net present value. This allows us to preserve the psychological benefits of expressing the answer as a relative measure, an IRR, while still accounting for the total value of the benefits in the absolute measure, the NPV. We should calculate the IRR on the incremental cash flows of each project versus the other possibility.

Line up the projects with the one requiring a larger investment on the left and the one requiring a smaller investment in the middle. Show the difference in the third column on the right. That column should show an incremental investment required as an outflow and incremental cash generated as inflows. When you calculate the IRR on the incremental cash flows, that shows the additional return obtained by increasing the investment from the smaller to the larger amount. If the IRR is above the cost of capital, that additional investment is justified by the additional return.

By the way, if you use the same cost of capital as the discount rate to calculate NPVs for each project, the NPV and incremental IRR will *always* give you the same answer for ranking decisions, just as the NPV and IRR *always* give you the same answer for selection/rejection decisions. The incremental IRR *must* exceed the cost of capital when the NPV on the larger project is higher. Similarly, the incremental IRR *must* be inadequate when the smaller project shows the higher NPV. Thus, these are merely two different methods of handling the same concept. We can either link the level of the return with the total magnitude of the total investment, or we can evaluate the portion attributable to the difference in the magnitudes of the two investments.

Obviously, by now, we have confused you enough that you could use an example:

Investment	Project A	Project B	Project C
Year 0	($2,000,000)	($100,000)	($1,900,000)
Year 1	430,000	30,000	400,000
Year 2	430,000	30,000	400,000
Year 3	430,000	30,000	400,000

Investment	Project A	Project B	Project C
Year 4	430,000	30,000	400,000
Year 5	430,000	30,000	400,000
Year 6	430,000	30,000	400,000
Year 7	430,000	30,000	400,000
Year 8	430,000	30,000	400,000
Year 9	430,000	30,000	400,000
Year 10	550,000	50,000	500,000
NPV @15%	$ 187,733	$ 55,507	$ 132,226
IRR	17.4%	27.9%	16.8%

As you can see, Project B has the highest IRR (28 percent), but Project A should be preferred, based upon its higher NPV ($188,000). Similarly, Project A's incremental IRR over Project B is 17 percent, which is greater than the 15 percent cost of capital and indicates the same preference for Project A for the same reason merely expressed in a different form.

Adjusting for Risk

You could now raise the very relevant issue of risk and other factors adjusting the required returns for one project more than another. Yet, the solution would merely be to use different discount rates to lower the NPV of Project A to account for any additional risk, or to raise the NPV for Project B to account for less risk than the average business upon which the 15 percent cost of capital was based. On a qualitative basis, the same factors could be used to evaluate the adequacy of the incremental IRR—such as, if the larger project is riskier than the smaller one, a 20 percent incremental IRR may be the proper benchmark, even though the cost of capital is only 15 percent.

Multiple Project Ranking

There is one real problem in using incremental IRR calculations to rank projects. What do you do with a large number of mutually exclusive projects to rank or in a situation of applying capital rationing to a large number of projects? For the former case, you could set up all the projects from left to right in descending order of investments and calculate each increment. Of course, using NPVs might be easier. For the latter case, where you are looking for maximum total return within the magnitude of the total capital available for investment, you really need to take all combinations of projects possible. Then either the NPVs for each combination, or the listing of each combination in descending order, will give you the correct answer. NPVs, however, should again be much easier to use. In practice, of course, you would probably need a computer to handle a capital rationing program within many projects. Then, NPVs and incremental IRRs can both be calculated to give the most information to the decision maker—such as your boss.

Capital Rationing Philosophy

What about *capital rationing* as a concept? Is it a good idea? Again, the subject is discussed in most textbooks, but we are not sure most people ever understand the implications. To be blunt, if you believe all that other stuff in the textbooks—such as developing an optimal capital structure with the lower cost of capital and then selecting all projects with risk-adjusting internal rates of return exceeding that capital cost—capital rationing is a bogus concept.

Let's take an extreme case as an example. On the one hand, all your investment bankers and commercial bankers tell you that you must reduce debt. Your debt/capital ratio is quite high, and you are borrowing at 50 percent over the prime rate, LIBOR, or any other benchmark. By definition, your cost-of-debt calculations will show a high-cost percentage. Also, your price/earnings ratio is low, and the market does not appear to have bought your investor-relation stories about the bright future prospects for the company that are just around the corner. Yet, your inside information shows these growth prospects to be quite real. In other words, based upon all of your growth estimates for the business, your cost-of-equity calculations will show a high-cost percentage. To sum up, your weighted average cost of capital appears to be very high—let's say in the 20 percent plus range, after taxes.

On the other hand, your business development group has come up with a new product that is better than warm bread. There is no one on your staff who does not feel that a 50 percent post-tax return is assured, and the upside potential is unlimited. In fact, this is the very inside information that makes your cost-of-equity calculations so high.

Now in the light of your high cost of capital, your CEO has circulated a memorandum implementing severe capital rationing. Once you spend enough to maintain your plants and equipment in the most minimal operating conditions, you have a small bankroll. The CEO does not want to see any projects that will cause him to exceed the capital rationing ceiling because he is finally going to tighten the corporate belt and get debt back in line in order to have some good progress to report at the next shareholders' meeting.

This is how capital rationing in the above situation would work:

- Forget about any optimal allocation of resources!
- Reduce the resources used at all costs!
- Forget 50 percent "guaranteed" returns!
- Refuse to raise any funds even to support such fantastic and safe projects at this time!

Without capital rationing in the above situation, we would still have some sticky issues to address and a lot of talking to do with all sorts of bankers and the "Street." They would explore various private placement opportunities and consider debt/equity hybrid instruments— such as high premium convertible bonds. The poor corporate image, however, could very easily mean that the marginal cost of capital for raising new funds to support the new high-return product line is 25 percent post-tax. Yet, the money can be raised at some cost.

Then, with the new product line funded and the high returns rolling in, the 25 percent cost of capital would more than be covered. The value of the company would increase. The stock price would rise, debt would be reduced, and borrowing rates would return to normal. The new cost of capital would also be properly reduced to a more normal 15 percent post-tax range.

Ranking under capital rationing may be a needed skill to learn in practice, but you should be aware that the fundamental impact on valuation is suboptimal if good projects are lost. So you are really optimally ranking within a suboptimal framework.

There are, of course, practical uses for capital rationing not necessarily discussed in the textbooks. Also, in practice, capital rationing is not an absolute policy, at least not at the decision-making level. It is often no more than an incentive to group, subsidiary, and division managers to eliminate all projects that are not absolutely necessary, even if the optimistic projections yield an adequate return. The corporate belt should be tightened, and our rose-colored-glass projects should be discounted more than usual. In other words, we can no longer afford to err on the optimistic side.

The executive co-author has lived through and implemented more than one type of capital rationing aimed at overly optimistic projections in more than one large, sophisticated corporation in different industries. Sometimes a capital expenditure ceiling was explicitly stated when the CEO or group president was certain that his line managers could not find many realistic high-return projects utilizing greater amounts of capital. Since he could not fully evaluate the relative optimism in each set of projections, capital rationing provided an incentive for the project sponsors to do so. Sometimes, hurdle rates well in excess of capital costs were utilized so as to remove at least some of the excess return forecasted.

The major problem we have seen with all such capital rationing mechanisms is that the accurate forecaster may lose a good project along with, or in place of, the project sponsor with an optimistic outlook for unintentionally erroneous or empire-building reasons. Nevertheless, even under the systems we have seen, we are sure that in most cases if a truly ''sure-bet,'' high-return project were proposed, senior management would usually consider making an exception.

Also, capital rationing will lend support to our efforts to get a refinancing plan implemented. It is quite important, when you tell the banks and the ''Street'' that you will be reducing debt and trying to limit capital spending, that you are believed. This does not mean there are no exceptions. The party line can certainly be rewritten, when necessary, to factor in a new product possibility and even an entirely new financial plan.

At CBS, for example, apart from any fallacious capital rationing, there have been many changes in our fundamental philosophies and financial needs. Higher debt leverage became acceptable during 1984 and 1985. Stock repurchases, generating two to three times the prior debt/capital levels, quickly resulted. Then in 1986 and 1987, the decision to liquidate some of our businesses was made (sometimes in response to sudden, surprisingly high purchase offers), resulting in sales of significant assets that generated surplus cash in excess of total debt. The verbal description of our treasury plans for financing and investments, therefore, turned around by 180 degrees.

Thus, capital rationing need not be a requirement as a treasury necessity to ensure that changes in financial plans and certain discussions with bankers do not occur. Nevertheless, one partial defense of the rationing concept is the assurance that about-faces in financial plans are warranted by fundamental changes (ones that are beyond merely finding more good capital projects than were included in the annual capital budget).

Summary and Conclusions

In terms of financial mistakes, we hope this chapter makes ranking of projects by NPVs or incremental IRRs less of a mathematical mystique and places the issue in a better perspective. Also, for one of the two major ranking situations—capital rationing, as opposed to mutual exclusivity—we hope we have outlined the problems arising from using it too broadly. Capital rationing should be treated as merely a practical exception to sound resource allocation to be used only in a limited fashion in practice.

CHAPTER 10

Joining and Separating Assets in the Valuation Process— Fission and Fusion

Introduction of Terms

No, you have not obtained any secret documents in this innocent book on finance that outline plans for some new nuclear weapon. The title of this chapter merely refers to the continuing process of identifying, analyzing, isolating, and combining two different types of elements that are the sources of profits in any business. These two elements are the *value of the assets*, on the one hand, and the *value of the overall business* or its segments, on the other hand.

Two growing phenomena exist in which a full understanding of this process and of the difference between these factors is most relevant. First, acquisitions of ongoing businesses with extensive asset liquidation value have already been discussed in terms of hostile takeovers and leveraged buyouts (see Chapters 8 and 20). Second, the use of joint ventures (combining asset and business values from different companies) in an attempt to survive together in the technologically-altered parameters of given industries has become a major source of growth.

Asset Values in Acquisitions

Asset values appear to have been resurrected as the primary measure of the value of many companies. (The basic logic behind this phenomenon is outlined in Chapter 4 on residual values.) They are obviously a measure of value to be considered, even if no liquidation, buyout, or other major event is planned. After all, to the extent plans change or business prospects diminish, the shareholders may ultimately gain or lose on the basis of the asset value. Now, in acquisition situations, the importance of asset values is often even more apparent. With respect to the takeover and leveraged-buyout phenomenon, as discussed in Chapters 8 and 20, the resale of assets and/or asset-based debt can provide the funds to pay for the acquisition. Even if a corporation is purchased as an ongoing business, the net cost of the purchase can be greatly reduced.

Let's take a look at a fast-food restaurant company whose stock is trading at book value and whose major assets consist of the following:

	Book Value (000)	Market Value (000)
• 100 Restaurants		
— Land	$ 2,000	$ 20,000
— Building	10,000	20,000
— Equipment, fixtures, and furniture	10,000	10,000
• Headquarters building		
— Land	8,000	25,000
— Building	10,000	25,000
• Television station	60,000	100,000
Total	$100,000	$200,000

Looking at these figures, you might wish to become a restaurateur—as long as *you* did not have to work 12 hours a day managing the restaurant itself. And if you had the $100 million your father-in-law told you your wife had, which could be the value of the target company, you might wish to buy the company, become chairman, and let the management do their thing. An even more enjoyable hypothetical situation would be one in which you could also recoup your $100 million investment immediately. How can you have your cake—or restaurant business—and eat it too?

Well, first, you would sell the TV station that generated only a small portion of the company's earnings, and remove it from your mainstream business. Second, you would transfer the restaurant land and buildings to an off-balance sheet real-estate company, which would be a joint venture between your company and another restaurant company contributing similar assets of similar value. The joint venture would immediately mortgage the restaurant real estate and distribute the cash to the two investing corporations. The real estate would be leased to the corporations to provide rental payments to cover the debt service. And finally, you would sell the headquarters building to a leasing firm in a sale/leaseback transaction.

There is an excellent chance you could obtain enough for your company to pay yourself a dividend in one form or another to recoup your investment, at least apart from taxes. The earnings of your company may be only moderately reduced due to the lost TV station profits and the rental payments. The value of your company should, however, be reduced more significantly. Yet, if it merely retained half of its original asset value, you would have obtained that value for nothing since your entire investment would have been returned to you.

One of the major mistakes in this area occurs when the financial press and some less-than-precise business executives fail to cite the decline in earnings and valuation. They act as if the company can be partially liquidated to recoup the entire investment, which is true, without any reduction in earnings or value, which is quite false. After all, sale/leasebacks do require rental payments, and sold businesses no longer provide earnings. (Let's not complicate matters with contingency payouts.) Also, just as important, once you realize the full difference between book values and market values, an additional reduction in valuation is likely, since the market had incorporated a portion of this liquidation possibility in its prior valuation. Yet, if you keep two-thirds of the earnings and one-half of the value for nothing, that is certainly a good deal.

If you were less greedy and did not need the $100 million to play with, but you were also a risk averter with tremendous self-doubt, the above asset values would still provide some fantastic benefits. Let's say this particular restaurant operation was still unproven and had not yet turned the corner into profitability. In this case, the type of assets you described above would provide a tremendous hedge for your bet.

The same sales of the major assets outlined above would generate the $100 million you paid for the company. If the restaurants never made any money and the business was later abandoned, you would merely need to break-even from the sale of the equipment and liquidation of the inventory (in terms of covering any trade payables and debt) in order to avoid a loss.

Given the asset market values of the real estate described in this case, most of it should be independent of the success or failure of the fast-food business itself, because this type of real estate—at least the land and basic buildings—is relatively fungible. Other fast-food and retail businesses should be able to utilize the land and buildings, though not the decor fixtures, without extensive modification. The asset values, therefore, can provide a significant downside cushion that may turn a risky business venture into a relatively safe one, even if you plan to run the business rather than go for a fast liquidation profit.

Joint Ventures

How about *joint ventures*? Fission and fusion can play an even greater role in understanding their economics.

First, much of the equity contribution by one or more joint-venture partners is in the form of assets, which must be valued separately, as outlined above. We must then project the income stream from the joint-venture operations that will utilize the assets.

Second, an even more likely candidate for some financial mistakes is the need for separation of the three decisions that result simultaneously in any joint venture. There is an acquisition decision for the assets, business, and management of the other investor. There is a divestiture decision for the assets, business, and management you are contributing or selling in part to the other investor. And there is a decision on the type of business and operating plans and related agreements providing the bylaws to run the joint venture together.

Let's describe the basic concept of *joint venture* (JV). Two or more partners contribute equity in the form of cash or assets, agree on what portions of their own businesses and/or management will be incorporated into the joint venture, and establish group rules for how different types of decisions will be made. The successful joint ventures seek to give the JV entity/operation a life of its own. Thus, ideally, one or all of the partners could ultimately withdraw, and the values created in establishing and developing the JV could still be maintained.

At the other extreme, some JVs are merely extensions of or pseudonyms for everyday operating agreements—supply contracts, maintenance contracts, marketing/distribution agreements, and so on. In these cases, a product and/or service is merely being sold, and there are accompanying obligations of the buyer and seller.

Naturally, even an independent JV can effectively utilize various operating agreements with any of the partners, but some degree of independence for every operating business decision must be included. Distinguishing between true joint ventures and operating contracts is obviously one element of misunderstanding in this area. More importantly, the failure to consider the independent JV as more than a mere operating agreement camouflages the fundamental acquisition, divestiture, and bylaws decisions that are actually being made.

If these decisions are all being made at once, then what complete and separate analysis must also be prepared to ensure that the decisions are made intelligently? Why of course, a *full acquisition analysis*, on the one hand, and a *full divestiture analysis* on the other hand.

In a 50/50 JV, for example, you are acquiring 50 percent of the assets and businesses that the other partner is contributing. What is the value of this 50 percent interest on a stand-alone basis, in terms of the present value of the future cash-flow stream and in terms of the liquidation value of the assets? Also, what is the true cost you are being charged, in terms of the value of your contribution, relative to your other opportunities to acquire the same type of assets and businesses needed to make a successful joint venture? These represent the financial evaluation of the acquisition and the opportunity-cost evaluation of mutually exclusive alternative acquisitions.

With respect to the cost being charged, it is based on the value of your own 50 percent contribution to you. It could be a straightforward investment of cash; but, it usually involves the contribution of assets and businesses. And how can such a contribution be valued? Why, with a divestiture analysis.

Such a divestiture analysis should be based on the present value of the 50 percent of the cash flows compared with the value of 50 percent of the acquisition cash flows. Also, analogous to the acquisition review, alternative prices available for a straight divestiture should be ascertained. These valuations represent the divestiture opportunity cost of retention or of sale outside the JV.

Finally, now that you have an acquisition value of what you are receiving and a divestiture value of what you should be receiving, then you must add some additional qualitative factors that apply specifically to joint ventures. Basically, they relate to the desirability and compatibility of the partner and to the workability of the joint-venture bylaws and operating procedures. Unlike an acquisition or divestiture, you cannot walk away from the seller or buyer, but must live with him to the extent of operating the business together. Ideally, there should be limited partner-level decisions required in the bylaws, but there can never be complete autonomy for most JVs with most corporations.

So you must ask a few questions. Is this the type of firm whose image would make one proud to be a partner? How about corporate culture and style? Is mine a buttoned-down, detail-oriented company, and are they a bunch of hip shooters and wheeler-dealers? Do we share the same goals and concern for the JV? Do we agree on the proper level of financing? Does the JV agreement give the management enough autonomy? Are there likely to be many or a few major negotiations required to reach the partner-level decisions outlined in the bylaws? Last, but not least, will the JV be able to achieve enough independence and continuity in the future to allow either partner to reap the benefits of their efforts?

Many of the joint ventures we have seen in practice did emphasize all three of the decisions. In addition to the more obvious acquisition decision (albeit with only a 50 percent interest), line managers have often been quite reluctant to divest half of their pride-and-joy business, even if it was in a startup stage. Moreover, the concept of working with most other corporations has been very frightening in some cases, and this situation is usually worsened as negotiations about procedures—to resolve disagreements on strategies, approve capital expansions, or liquidate assets—progress during the contract drafting and closing process.

Many of you may have seen only a combined analysis of joint ventures, where the present value of half of the projected cash flows might be compared with the present value of 100 percent cash flows from retaining the assets to be contributed to the JV. Well, even we concur that this calculation should be done in addition to the above analysis to summarize the two most obvious, mutually exclusive alternatives—investing in the JV or merely not investing in the JV. *If* all the other alternatives have also been fully analyzed and properly eliminated from consideration, then this summary calculation will also emphasize the net effect, at least, of the acquisition and divestiture analyses, as discussed above. Yet, that's a big "if," and we feel it will not hold in most cases.

Let's take a look at Table 10-1, which gives a numerical example for a 50/50 joint venture and some alternatives.

Suppose there has been a decision made by Partner 1 that a JV was necessary, given overall capital needs and technological positions. Assume Partner 1 can neither retain his contribution in column 1 or acquire another business in columns 2 and 3. Assume there are no economies of scale, synergies, or taxes to be identified. Then Partner 1 must overpay with his own contribution in column 1 for Partner 2's contribution in column 4. So the value of a 50 percent share of the JVs in column 6 is not as good as column 1, but it is still good enough for Partner 1. Also, Partner 2 receives more value in column 7 than Partner 1's evaluation of Partner 2's opportunity cost in column 4, and Partner 2 receives more than Partner 1 in column 6.

Summary and Conclusions

Asset values can provide a significant downside cushion to a business. The market value of an asset, such as land and buildings, should be independent of the business itself. Proper valuation of fungible assets can demonstrate the potential for increasing the total return and enhancing liquidity. These can then be realized later through liquidation, sale/leasebacks, or contributions to joint ventures of various components of the company.

Table 10-1. Acquisition Alternatives

Year	Partner 1 Contribution (1)	Acquired Business (2)	Combined Business (3)	Partner 2 Contribution (4)	Joint Venture (5)	Partner 1 Share (6)	Partner 2 Share (7)
0	($ 100)*	($ 150)	($ 250)	($ 90)**	($ 190)	($ 100)	($ 90)
1	20	25	45	16	36	18	18
2	20	25	45	16	36	18	18
3	20	25	45	16	36	18	18
4	20	25	45	16	36	18	18
5	20	25	45	16	36	18	18
6	20	25	45	16	36	18	18
7	20	25	45	16	36	18	18
8	20	25	45	16	36	18	18
9	20	25	45	16	36	18	18
10	220	330	550	176	396	198	198
Net present values at @15%	$ 49.8	$ 50.9	$ 100.7	$ 29.9	$ 79.7	$ 34.8	$ 44.8

*Divestiture alternative net proceeds is opportunity-cost investment for Partner 1.
**Acquisition alternative value placed on Partner 2 contribution by Partner 1.

With respect to joint ventures there are three major reasons to separate acquisition and divestiture analysis; we will state these reasons in ascending order of priority. First, without the separation, you cannot see the simultaneous acquisition and loss of a piece of the action. Second, by knowing what your potential partner's contribution is worth, you have a better idea of some of his opportunity costs and a better idea of market-price benchmarks (these factors are usually implicitly or explicitly part of the negotiations). Third, and most importantly, only a full understanding of the acquisition and divestiture elements will allow you to identify and evaluate all of your own opportunity costs, in the form of other acquisition and divestiture opportunities for the same type of assets and business, and all of the economic and legal issues that are usually part of acquisition/divestiture reviews (which are equally applicable to joint ventures).

The financial press will usually cite three other reasons as the driving force behind joint ventures. First, *diversification and spreading of risk* means you need not bet as much yourself for any new business developed via the joint-venture approach. Second, *conservation of capital* means you have less capital committed to this business, leaving more for your other businesses and/or to delay any changes in your overall debt and equity financing plans. (Please note that capital rationing underlies this concept; we discussed only limited justifications for capital rationing in Chapter 9.) Third, *broadening of expertise* needed for new businesses may obviously be obtainable if another company has experience, skills, patents, or a marketing/production infrastructure in place in one or more of the related areas.

The above are all very important considerations. In fact, we fully concur that broadening of expertise has become a requisite for entering many of the new fields created by technological change, especially where two or more separate, older industries are being merged—for example, several of the new entertainment, information, and telecommunication businesses, such as the CBS/Fox joint venture for video-cassette films and programs and the CBS/IBM/Sears joint venture for videotext electronic information, home shopping, and so on.

Yet, let us also state that in no way are these other considerations inconsistent with the acquisition/divestiture approach to joint analysis.

While they represent important qualitative factors to be considered, or even the main purpose for a given joint venture, a full financial analysis is still required, and the acquisition/divestiture approach plays a critical role in that analysis for all of the reasons discussed above.

CHAPTER 11

An Evaluation Model
for Foreign Capital Projects

International Factors and Corporate Philosophy

When we leave the confines of our own nation and its economic system, determining the relevant financial measures and methodology becomes much more difficult. Domestic financial analysis can appear to be child's play by comparison when we wrestle with the problems of the proper approach to international financial decisions. It is as if all our known words and criteria must be redefined. This is just as true for the full evaluation process to be used with respect to international capital expenditure as it is for the profit return calculations discussed in Chapter 7.

Thus, we must specifically define, or redefine, several key elements in the standard capital evaluation model based on the net present value of cash flows. The basic approach is the same—namely, to choose the maximum net present value calculated at the risk-adjusted cost of capital. Yet each element of the calculation must be defined in a manner that will yield results on a comparable basis to those of domestic projects. Even more of a problem, before we can start on the specific definitions, we must first determine our company's philosophy with respect to their international operations.

- Is our corporation a domestic U.S. company with some foreign operations?

  Are the foreign operations viewed as temporary investments, with the ultimate goal being the repatriation of the profits to the U.S. to fund domestic investment or dividends to domestic shareholders?

- Or are the international operations part of a permanent program to allocate our resources in an optimal manner among business opportunities in all or most countries around the world?

  Is the goal to reinvest as much money in each foreign operation as can be done so profitably and to remit additional profits to any country where the maximum risk-adjusted returns can be earned?

In other words, is our company a domestic corporation with ancillary, temporary foreign activity? Or is it a truly multinational corporation in outlook, with a worldwide investment game plan?

While most non-U.S. multinational companies have little difficulty in maintaining the multinational perspective, we have seen many American controllers, treasurers, and boards of directors (as well as some international finance textbooks) espouse a more parochial domestic attitude. In practice, once significant ex-U.S. operations are fully established in the form of subsidiaries, a multinational approach is usually incorporated into the organization chart and overall corporate financial procedures. Yet even in such cases, there may be a constant struggle to maintain that multinational outlook in establishing the precise analytical requirements for capital projects and in having them accepted in senior management reviews of major capital-project and acquisition proposals.

The answer to this question of philosophy will impact on three or four of the definitions for the major elements in the net present value calculation.

Defining Cash Flow

The first of the four present value elements is the one most obviously affected—what is cash flow?

- More specifically, are cash outflows only those funds transferred from the U.S. to fund investment requirements?
- Are cash inflows only those proceeds remitted to the U.S.?

For the multinational, the answers would be negative for both questions. Cash flows for international capital projects would be defined in the same manner as those for domestic projects. All cash outflows from both debt and equity sources and all cash inflows to or from the company or its consolidated subsidiaries anywhere in the world would be included.

For a domestic corporation, however, both answers could easily be affirmative, and some changes in our net present value model would be required. For a domestic company philosophy, an overly liberal view of local borrowing and an overly conservative view of income could result. Such a philosophy would likely lead to consideration of only cash flows to and from the U.S. as being relevant. The incurrence of local foreign debt, therefore, to fund most of a project's needs, would have no impact on defined cash flow, since no outflow from the U.S. would be required. Yet for all consolidated subsidiaries, the debt would actually be reflected on the balance sheet, so the incremental effect on the corporation's debt capacity would be understated. Similarly, no income earned locally would be considered as a cash inflow until a dividend, royalty, or transfer-price payment was made. Yet, for consolidated subsidiaries, this would understate earnings that would actually be reported on the consolidated income statement.

If we take the domestic company approach, perhaps there is an analogy to analyses done on a leveraged basis, where only cash flows to and from our equity position in the U.S. are incorporated in the present value calculations. Yet, if these were used, then the hurdle rate or risk-adjusted cost of capital must be increased to the higher cost of equity because the lower cost of debt is already incorporated into the local borrowing. There must also be an exception for any local debt guaranteed by the parent company in the U.S., since that would be treated as part of the U.S. debt structure by the creditors and rating agencies. Finally, there is an overall distortion in using a leveraged approach for any consolidated subsidiary because the inclusion of local foreign debt on the consolidated balance sheet will diminish the amount of U.S. debt capacity available for an optimal capital structure. (See Chapter 20.)

For deconsolidated countries, where remittance of currency payments to the U.S. is blocked, perhaps both definitions of cash flow and both approaches are relevant. In the long run, the cumulative cash flows should be the same, unless funds become blocked permanently; the latter is really a risk. The timing, however, can be very different for all cash outflows and inflows. Two net present values, therefore, calculated on both the multinational and domestic company bases, should be prepared to provide the additional needed information for the decision maker.

In practice, even when first establishing new subsidiaries in less developed countries, the risk of blocked funds is quite apparent. We have seen two sets of financials:

- One prepared on the total cash flows in the developing country; and
- One prepared on cash flows from the developing country to the U.S. to be presented to senior management of at least one company in evaluating such expansion programs.

One last point on cash flows should be mentioned. If a foreign operation is being proposed, be sure to calculate all the incremental cash flows attributable to U.S. operations supplying the new subsidiary with product and management technology. These often represent significant, hidden benefits of the project. By the same token, if an export and/or licensee operation is being converted to a full-blown local subsidiary, be sure to deduct any export cash flows lost in the incremental analyses to avoid double counting.

Redefining Tax Rates

Moving right along to the next element of our present value calculations, what is the relevant tax rate to use? Under a domestic company approach, the answer is simple: U.S. tax rates should be applied to net cash remittances to the U.S. For the multinational company, however, we must count the proverbial angels on the head of that proverbial pin.

For a U.S.-based multinational company, the ultimate tax rate had been the U.S. rate (net of foreign tax credits) upon repatriation of the income and other payments. Also, even if the funds were "repatriated" through other foreign subsidiaries and were used for investment in other foreign countries, the U.S. rates might have been the best estimate of the average rates to be paid when funds were returned to the company for worldwide investment needs, rather than local, one-country usage. The only problem, of course, was one of timing. If lower rates were paid in foreign countries for ten years, the time value of the deferred taxes was not accounted for. Yet, this was the least of the distortions among which we had to choose.

In the "good old days," from at least one point of view, many foreign tax rates were below U.S. rates and some significant operations could easily funnel profits into tax-heaven countries. For at least one highly controversial acquisition, representing a major new-product-line expansion, the lower average tax rates for about half of the profit derived from foreign sources become a major issue. Not only was the reliance on non-U.S. revenue a problem for some of the American management teams, but the tax rates were of temporary and/or fictitious benefit. On the other hand, the division sponsors could not understand why there was any problem in showing the high post-tax increase in the cash flows. In this case, we feel the use of the U.S. tax rates by the corporate staff was warranted, though an upside of tax deferrals for higher earlier cash flows should also have been considered.

Please note, however, that foreign rates are now lower and excess foreign tax credits exist (which is now true for most companies under the new U.S. tax law), so the local foreign taxes may be the only ones to ever get paid. If the foreign rates are above the U.S. rates, then additional tax credits will be generated upon repatriation of the earning. These credits, though, will merely add to the excess and be of no value. If the foreign rates are below the U.S. rates, then additional U.S. tax liabilities will also be generated, but excess credits will always be available to offset them.

Incorporating Inflation and Foreign Exchange Rates

The third element of the present value calculations affected by the international issues is the combination of inflation and foreign exchange rates. For either a domestic or international company, both of these factors must be projected in order to obtain dollar-equivalent cash flows and to use a dollar-equivalent cost of capital as a hurdle rate, albeit one that is adjusted as described below. Using local-currency projections and a local-currency cost of capital for a U.S.-based company would entail some very difficult and subjective estimates. The practical solution, however, is to project neither inflation nor foreign exchange, but merely use U.S. inflation rates for all local sales and cost projections expressed as dollar equivalents at today's exchange rate.

In the long run, such as a 15-year life of capital project, the foreign exchange-rate fluctuations should be a function of the differences in inflation rates that make one currency more or less valuable. In other words, relative purchasing power will be maintained so that higher inflation in one currency will be offset by a lower exchange rate for that currency. This concept is the familiar one of purchasing-power parity.

The following is an example of taking inflation into account in an exchange-rate calculation:

Example 1: Purchasing-Power Parity

A. Assumptions:
Year 1

$$\$1.00 = LCY\ 1.00$$
$$1\ widget\ cost\ \$1.00$$
$$1\ widget\ cost\ LCY\ 1.00$$

Year 10

$$1\ widget\ cost\ \$2.00$$
$$1\ widget\ cost\ LCY\ 1.50$$
$$\$1.00 = LCY\ 0.75$$

B. Inflation:

$$\text{Inflation in \$} \quad = 100\%$$
$$\text{Inflation in LCY} \quad = 50\%$$

C. Exchange Rate:

$$\text{\$ devaluation} \quad = 25\%$$
$$\text{LCY appreciation} = 33\%$$

D. Relationships:

$$\text{New FX rate of \$/LCY} = \text{Initial FX rate} \times \left(\frac{1 + \text{\$ inflation}}{1 + \text{LCY inflation}} \right)$$

$$\left(\frac{\$1.00}{\text{LCY } 1.00} \right) \times \left(\frac{1.00 + 1.00}{1.00 + 0.50} \right) = \left(\frac{2.00}{1.50} \right) = \frac{\$1.33}{\text{LCY } 1.00}$$

Therefore, LCY is worth 133%, or 33% more.

$$\text{New FX rate of LCY/\$} = \text{Initial rate of LCY per \$} \times \left(\frac{1 + \text{LCY inflation}}{1 + \text{\$ inflation}} \right)$$

$$\left(\frac{\text{LCY } 1.00}{\$1.00} \right) \times \left(\frac{1.00 + 0.50}{1.00 + 1.00} \right) = \left(\frac{1.50}{2.00} \right) = \left(\frac{\text{LCY } 0.75}{\$1.00} \right)$$

Therefore, $ is worth only 75%, or 25% less.

Using alternative methods of forecasting both exchange rates and local inflation rates could, therefore, be considered redundant since in the long term, inflation differentials are the most widely used bases for forecasting exchange rates. Forward-market rates also certainly could be used, and they are based upon interest-rate differentials. Yet, for the long term, the forward rates are not readily available, and interest-rate differential forecasts are usually based upon inflation differentials anyway, as shown by the *interest-rate parity* and the *Fisher effect* in the following example:

Example 2: Interest-Rate Parity and Fisher Effect

A. Interest-Rate Components/Calculation:

$ inflation	=	100%
LCY inflation	=	50%
Real returns	=	50%

$ interest	=	[(100% + $ inflation) × (100% + real return)] − 100%
LCY interest	=	[(100% + LCY inflation) × (100% + real return)] − 100%
$ interest	=	(200% × 150%) − 100% = 200%
LCY interest	=	(150% × 150%) − 100% = 125%

B. Interest-Rate Parity:

$ discount % per arithmetic i.r. differential %
= ($i.r. − LCY i.r.)/(100% + LCY i.r.)
= (200% − 125%)/(100% + 125%) = 75/225 = 33%

$ discount %/forward-market rate compounded
= (100% + 200%)/(100% + 125%) − 100% = 33%

C. Fisher Effect:

$ discount % = LCY appreciation % of initial
exchange rate (from Example 1)* = 33%

Synthesis

1. *Purchasing-power parity*—The expected future exchange rate is a function of the inflation differential (Example 1).

2. *Interest-rate components/calculation*—The interest-rate differential is a function of the inflation differential (Example 2A).

---

*$ discount % = LCY appreciation % (not $ depreciation %)
   = Expected increase in $ obtained per unit of LCY
 $ premium % = LCY depreciation % (not $ appreciation %)
   = Expected decrease in $ obtained per unit of LCY

3. *Fisher effect*—The expected future exchange rate is a function of the interest-rate differential (Example 2C).

4. *Interest-rate parity*—The forward rate is a function of the interest-rate differential (Example 2B).

5. *Synthesis*—The expected future exchange rate is a function of the forward rate (3 and 4 above), which is a function of the interest-rate differential (3 and 4 above), which in turn is a function of the inflation differential (1 and 2 above).

Redefining Hurdle Rates and Costs of Capital

The fourth element of the present value calculations affected by international issues is the most complex. What *hurdle rate* or *cost of capital* should be used? Here we must go to the fundamental factors affecting the components of the cost of capital themselves, as discussed in Chapter 16.

The cost-of-debt differences can be estimated easily by comparing local-currency interest rates adjusted for exchange-rate changes, using forward-market rates and/or inflation differentials to obtain dollar-equivalent interest rates. For most hard currencies, the rates should be similar to U.S. interest rates. For some Latin American countries, the dollar-equivalent rates could be high, based upon risk factors.

Occasionally, real interest rates in a given country can be relatively high or low, apart from risk levels. Temporary imbalances in the supply and demand of a fund or a specific central bank policy may be causal factors; as an example, Argentina's shift from negative real interest after foreign exchange-rate adjustments in 1985, to a high-positive real interest rate in 1986. In such cases, only if non-local debt funding of the local subsidiary were possible (probably through intercompany loans), or if the local capital structure or capital requirements generated no debt, should the lower, risk-adjusted U.S. interest rates be used for the cost-of-debt component of the capital costs.

The cost-of-equity differences must reflect the greater risk factors that bear on an equity investment. If there is a local stock market, the risk premium for equity versus debt can be estimated and compared with

93

the same premium in U.S. stock markets. Then that premium can be added to the local dollar-equivalent cost of debt to fund the average cost of equity to be used. Specific adjustments for our own company and/or business (such as our own Beta factors) can be applied to obtain the relevant cost of equity for our firms for a given country.

Finally, the risk of currency becoming blocked can be accounted for by an additional risk adjustment. This may be more relevant for a non-resident company and, therefore, not fully reflected in the local market risk premiums. Even a multinational outlook should incorporate some risk premium for currency usage limited to only one country whose reinvestment needs may not adequately grow to utilize all funds generated. Nigeria is a good example. Many companies wanting to expand in Africa have recently been hurt there, and letters of credit are often required by sellers and rarely available on a non-recourse basis at the international banks.

For whatever reasons, however, most of the companies we have seen that use, or are considering, multiple hurdle rates for different countries, do require significantly higher returns for Latin America and other less-developed areas. Brazil and Argentina, for example, have been prime investment candidates at points in time for many American companies; however, disappointing results have caused some to shut down their operations. Any new investments, therefore, usually require higher than normal incremental returns.

However, there is one common error. While interest rates are a part of the hurdle-rate adjustment, many people feel that this differential, by itself, can merely be added to the cost of capital. Yet, these interest-rate differentials alone are inadequate for two reasons, as discussed above. First, only dollar-equivalent interest differentials are relevant, so interest rates must be adjusted for exchange-rate trends. Second, much of the riskiness of investments may be relegated to equity ownership versus creditor positions—although the latter have recently proven to be "quite risky" for major U.S. bank loans to Latin America. (While the actual losses on these loans are near zero so far, the creditors are nevertheless locked in for a long duration. Of course, they continue to earn market returns if interest is ever paid.)

Overall Assessment of International Expansion

Returning to some more philosophical matters, is the incorporation of foreign capital investments in the company's overall portfolio good or bad? Does it help promote high-return opportunities, and/or does it reduce risk through diversification? Well, in terms of profitability, there are a myriad of factors that are cited in an infinite number of books and articles on whether or not a firm can or should attempt to compete in international and/or foreign markets. Yet, we feel they basically boil down to merely two points.

First, do significant market opportunities exist for the company's products and services outside of the U.S. that can increase the size and growth of the company at profitable returns on the incremental investments in fixed and working capital?

Second, does a U.S.-based parent bring enough to the party to operate effectively in international and/or foreign markets? For example, a purely labor-intensive, non-technological, service business could give all of the edge to a local company. Naturally, the analysis and assumptions behind the present value calculations should focus on these issues and their subcomponents.

Perhaps a more interesting topic for discussion is the effects on overall risk. On the one hand, any multinational company is likely to be involved in at least some countries where political and economic risk exceeds those of the U.S. On the other hand, does the diversification of political and economic risk in general, by operating in several countries, reduce overall risk levels? Perhaps the real test should be the risk premium required by the stock market for multinational versus domestic firms.

If country diversification is a variable concept, then opportunities can arise to increase worldwide returns without comparable increases in risk. Portfolio theory tells us that if the risks are not highly correlated in the same direction, then the inclusion of several risky projects (or in this case, countries) can be done without increasing the overall investment portfolio risk. Since such risky countries may offer opportunities for very high returns, then this could be a way to increase worldwide returns for a given business or company without sacrificing overall safety. The actual experiences of many companies in Latin America, recent pullouts from South Africa, and the Latin American debt problem, however, may not give us comfort in international diversification. Risk reduction is a function of specific elements in a given portfolio and, therefore, simply expanding internationally in and of itself may not reduce risk.

Higher Leverage and Lower Interest-Rate Potential

Let's complete this chapter with a discussion of some potential exceptions or side issues to the basic approach to international capital expenditure evaluations. First, we have cited a risk-adjusted cost of capital, based upon worldwide capital structure. Yet, as every good international treasurer knows, the capital structure for foreign subsidiaries should often be more highly leveraged than any worldwide optimal debt ratio—which is an exception to Chapter 20.

The higher debt levels mean that as money is earned, it will be less likely to build up excess cash due to lack of repatriation opportunities— lack of dividend remittance capacity, blocked-funds situations, lack of intercompany loan repayment approvals, and so on. The debt, especially local foreign debt, can be repaid without any such approvals or remittance procedures.

In other words, this could be considered de facto repatriation, as excess cash of a consolidated subsidiary is employed to reduce the debt and total capital levels for the consolidated financial statements of the parent company. Thus, the local capital structure used to fund the capital expenditures could be much higher in debt than the worldwide average.

Nevertheless, even where local capital structures are more highly leveraged at the time capital expenditures are made, the worldwide capital structure is still the only relevant one. The consolidated statement of the parent will determine the financing costs. The worldwide cost of capital, therefore, is still the only one to use as a benchmark and should be adjusted merely for local interest rates and equity-risk levels, as previously outlined.

There is another situation, however, in which a different cost of capital should be used for specific debt situations. A multinational firm can borrow cheap funds as a result of local government subsidiaries, or may be forced to borrow more expensive funds as a result of local government restrictions. These capital rates should lower or raise the cost of capital, respectively.[1]

The difference in the post-tax cost of debt, based upon the interest differential multiplied by the worldwide percentage of debt in the total capital-funds mix, represents the adjustment to be made to the cost of capital. Unlike the local capital structure, this effect will not be removed when the consolidated balance is analyzed by rating agencies, investors, and so on, but instead this will represent a true change in the borrowing costs. Thus, the benefit or burden can and should be directly attributed to the specific capital expenditures that generate it by adjusting the hurdle rate for these expenditures.

Summary and Conclusions

As you can see, we have never really strayed from the basics of capital budgeting techniques when evaluating international capital expenditures. Yet, as the chapter title suggests, we need a rather comprehensive dictionary of terms just to be able to apply the basics in the international arena. Also, we need a fairly sophisticated analysis of the alternative definitions and approaches available for each of these terms. This will allow us to define each term in the manner most consistent with the same capital budgeting and financial valuation concepts that underlie the basic approach used for a one-country situation.

To sum up the approach recommended for a multinational company, the four elements of our net present value calculations affected by international issues can be handled as follows:

- *Cash flow*—All cash inflows and outflows from the company, anywhere in the world, including all consolidated debt incurred, should be included.
- *Tax rates*—The U.S. tax rate is probably most relevant to be applied

[1]Carter and Rodriquez, "International Budgeting," *International Finance Handbook*, Sec. 8.5, pp. 26-27.

to all worldwide pre-tax earnings for a U.S.-based parent corporation.

- *Inflation rates*—The U.S. inflation projections can be applied to all revenue and cost figures, with adjustments made for specific factors, such as price elasticity, margin erosion, and so on. Yet, neither local inflation rates nor future exchange-rate fluctuations need to be projected.

- *Hurdle rate*—An adjusted cost of capital should be prepared for each type of business in each country.

In practice, the only element that should cause a problem in calculations is the hurdle-rate adjustment. Calculating risk-adjusted costs of equity can be very difficult for a country's overall equity investment. Further adjustments for your firm's own product line can be even more difficult. Relatively standard hurdle rates, therefore, may be the best solution to use; they can be estimated for many countries. There are also services available to categorize and quantify risk levels by country.

Even more preferable is to calculate internal rates of return, and not present values. Then, for a given business in a given country, the decision makers can decide whether or not a given IRR return is adequate. For example, a 20 percent return is probably inadequate for Argentina and is probably more than adequate for most businesses in Canada. For many investment decisions, no more precision may be required to come up with the obvious correct answer.

PART II

CAPITAL MARKET ANALYSIS
FOR INVESTORS AND BORROWERS

CHAPTER 12

Pervasive Speculation

Definitions

Have you heard speculation being discussed as if it were the eighth deadly sin, or at least the breach of the 11th commandment? Has speculation been cited as a piece of childish idiocy, or as the practice of a naive gambler about to be taken in? Well, perhaps that is the problem in understanding this approach that is used by so many financial managers for numerous financial decisions.

For if speculation is such a dirty word, and most corporate executives, bankers, and investors are not so dirty or naive, then they cannot be involved in speculation. Yet, speculation is neither an evil or stupid practice on the one hand, nor a rarity among senior corporate executives, bankers, and investors on the other.

Every time a Ph.D. economist forecasts future economic conditions that differ from the consensus, every time a corporate treasurer forecasts future interest rates or foreign exchange rates, and every time a brokerage firm forecasts future stock prices, then we have a speculation. When we project results that differ from the market consensus and raise the prospects of beating the market—such as any one of the components of the capital or currency markets—we are speculating. Thus, speculation can be done by the best people for the best purposes and in the most prudent manner.

A corporate treasurer, for example, needs to manage exposures in foreign currencies incurred by his operating management colleagues. He also needs to decide when to borrow—at current or future interest rates—and whether or not this is a good time to float some additional equity. To satisfy these requirements, he hires several Ph.D.s in economics and finance, as well as subscribing to several of the best consulting and forecasting services in the foreign exchange and capital markets. Finally, he never follows extreme positions. He will only act in accordance with a consensus of forecasters and will even then hedge his bets, such as the practice of taking out forward contracts to cover only 50 percent of his receivables. Is the approach used by these responsible individuals "prudent," "moderate," and "well educated"? Of course! Well, then it is certainly not speculation, right? Wrong!

Speculation is merely the reliance upon forecast results that differ from the consensus that is implicit in the market itself. In other words, *speculation* is any attempt to beat the market on foreign exchange, interest rates, stock prices, and so on.

Speculation versus the Efficient Market

Now, if speculation is not a dirty word, does it make sense? The markets we have been citing, currency and capital (both debt and stock), are generally considered to be quite efficient. The definition of *efficient* under the hypothesis of the same name is:

> "All information is already included in the price of securities so you cannot beat the market over the long run by investing in those securities."

There are three common variations of the definition of this *efficient market hypothesis*:

- *Weak form*—All the price and volume information on securities that demonstrates a market trend is already reflected in the market prices, so you cannot beat the market by merely plotting this data and attempting to identify turning points. In other words, woe to all the technical analysts.

102

- *Semi-strong form*—All publicly-available information, including analysts' reports, newsletters, and so on, is already incorporated in the prices, so you cannot beat the market by being a good analyst or an avid reader. In other words, woe to security analysts and financial advisory services, or at least to their clients, unless the study merely helps select good portfolios in which to participate and does not try to beat the market.

- *Strong form*—Even insider information is already included in the market price. In other words, woe to all industrial espionage services.

The general consensus and empirical studies support the semi-strong form of the *efficient market hypothesis*. It appears, therefore, that the only way to beat the market is with inside information, not sophisticated analysis. The latter is already incorporated into the market prices and rates of return, including risk adjustments.

The good news is that you can obtain a profit by merely buying and selling at the market prices for your own reasons, such as an annual investment plan or to cover all foreign exchange invoices payable. Yet, the bad news is that you cannot beat the market without inside information.

Inside Information Requirement

Perhaps we better take a look at what is and what is not inside information for this purpose. How about security analyst reports, stock investor newsletters, foreign exchange advisory newsletters, interest-rate forecasts in the *Wall Street Journal*, and so on? No, since these are already factored into the market prices.

How about your own superb analysis of the relevant data in various company, S.E.C. and Wall Street reports? No, since a whole host of analysts have already figured this, and it has been factored into the market prices.

How about advice from your major banks, investment banks, or others? Well, if the advice is based upon private statements by a central banker on foreign exchange-related data or information, or upon confidential information about merger negotiations, these are at least candidates for the "inside information" designation. Yet, even with confidential information, you must be careful.

We know of two examples where one trade newsletter obtained inside information on a media acquisition. The first time they rumored that the deal negotiations were underway and progressing; it was at that exact point in time that months of negotiations had temporarily been terminated. The second time, they reported the unannounced price for the same deal at twice the price that was actually being paid.

Implications for the Investor

Assuming we cannot beat the market without inside information, and recognizing that the latter is quite hard to come by, what are the implications? Generally, you must avoid market transactions based upon any position or forecasts with respect to exchange rates, interest rates, and stock prices. As an investor, avoid the foreign exchange markets because there is no return to be earned apart from speculative gains.

Yet, be aware that the overall long-term returns in the stock market are good, so there is no need to be concerned with beating the market, but merely with participating at your own desired risk level. Perhaps this can be achieved via mutual funds, which come very close to the overall market average returns without most of the effort involved in constructing your own portfolios. If liquidity needs or risk aversion are abnormally high, then money market instruments or bonds may be the answer, though the returns are obviously much lower for these securities than equity stocks.

There are some additional implications of the efficient market hypothesis on stock market investment strategies. If you merely pick the recent winners or stocks currently in favor, is that a good idea? No, because in an efficient market, the impact of favorable trends is already reflected in the increased stock prices. How about merely eliminating the worst losers from the portfolio? Believe it or not, there is some empirical evidence to suggest this works. Perhaps there is a fringe element of the investment community that is less efficient in a relatively efficient market. In any case, we never said "efficient" meant "perfect."

The other common strategies relate to timing. Is it good to invest only when the market has declined? Again, trends and forecasts are taken into account in the market, so this should not work. Are stocks a safe bet in "bull markets" and should bonds be preferred in "bear markets?" Well, again, the market adjusts risk for each type of activity and accounts for trends in both the bond and stock segments, so this has not proven to be a good tool. Finally, dollar averaging has been proposed as a means of reducing costs per share bought, but that cannot work because you would still have the same dollar investment made at any given point regardless of the number of shares. The former, not the latter, represents the risk and opportunity of the investment.

Foreign Exchange Exposure Management

As a corporate financial officer or advisor, as opposed to an investor, one also should follow guidelines about how to avoid taking positions on market forecasts. The foreign exchange markets probably provide the best examples.

First of all, define foreign exchange exposure as that which concerns your economic/cash exposure, income statement exposure, or both. Second, obtain data on the amounts of these exposures in each currency. This is no simple task. Then, hedge all or none of such exposures. *Hedging*, of course, usually means taking out forward contracts in all currencies where such a market exists. Finally, avoid selective hedging, which is really another form of speculation. In other words, do not select which contracts to purchase or which ones to close out early based upon your outlook for the dollar or a given foreign currency. All your actions, both on the front end and during the life of the contract, should be aimed at neutralizing the exchange rates.

We still get a good laugh when we read foreign exchange newsletters that state, "Hedge 50 percent of your payables." It's like saying, "Let's remove 50 percent of the tumors that may be cancerous and wait to see if the other 50 percent will kill you at a slower rate." The costs of such a hedging program are unbelievably small, apart from the accounting/information systems and infrastructure that may or may not be in place. The bank spreads, implicit in their contract prices, can be no more than $1,000 per million dollars of contract value.

Likewise, when someone asks you for exchange-rate forecasts for profit budgets and similar purposes, merely use the forward-market rates, if they are available. There is some empirical evidence that some sophisticated, consensus forecasts are better prediction tools, but how do we know which ones to use? Conceptually, the difference may merely be an additional risk-aversion element in the forward-market pricing implicit in the spot rate or interest rates that determine this pricing. That is not inherent, though, in the pure forecasting models. In any case, you may wish to include such a risk factor in your own forecasts. It is difficult to isolate that currency risk from the other factors, and we do not know how to select which of the thousands of consensus forecasts can beat the implicit consensus of the market participants who set the forward-market prices.

Interest-Rate and Debt Strategies

For the corporate financial officer or advisor, there is also analo-gous advice for selecting the timing, maturities, and fixed/floating rate terms of debt borrowings. Again, you must avoid acting upon interest-rate outlooks. The market outlook is already embodied in the long-term rates that are basically a geometric average of current and expected short-term rates. Thus, you cannot beat the market by going short term or by designating floating rates when long-term rates are high, or by locking in long term when short-term rates are expected to rise.

In general, fixed rates should be utilized when they are available. Maturities should be set to tie in with the period for which the borrowing is needed in order to avoid excess capitalization that would reduce the returns and increase debt ratios, as discussed in Chapters 2 and 13. When financing requirements are uncertain, fluctuating, or seasonal, then short-term debt should be used. Many large corporations utilize commercial paper extensively for this flexibility, but smaller firms may not be able to launch a successful commercial paper program.

Debt versus Equity Decisions

In choosing between debt and equity financing or in selecting the optimal time to float new stock, deferral of the equity issues is quite common when either the overall market or the company's stock has declined in value. Yet, are we trying to beat the market as equity by such delays, which would be the flip-side of the mistake just discussed vis-à-vis investors? Well, the answer is yes, unless we can justify the deferral on either of two bases that do not involve speculation on stock-price trends.

Our first rationale is the calculation of a higher optimal debt/capital ratio at the existing costs of the equity and costs of debt. After a stock-price decline, it is possible that this can occur when costs of equity increase much more rapidly than costs of debt. By definition, the optimal capital structure is that which yields the lowest weighted average cost of capital. Yet, the key to ensuring this is to keep asking yourself, "Would I defer an equity issue even if I knew my stock were priced fairly and would not rise disproportionately in the future?"

Our second rationale is our old friend *inside information*. If one of the company's secret projects will make millions, and the market either has not been told or does not believe it, corporate managers could certainly possess the best type of inside information. To avoid the risk of another mere rationalization, however, we can ask ourselves another question, "Would we make the same decision on deferral if we were stock market investors who were not privy to the corporate plans and projections?"

A typical example of misunderstanding on this subject is an article which appeared in the *Wall Street Journal* in the late 1970s. The article summarized the decline in stock-paid acquisition activity and cited the depressed stock market, which reduced the price/earnings ratios of the acquiring companies, as the causal factor. Yet, if the seller is also a publicly-traded corporation, there should be no effect. Only if the seller is privately held, or if the market fails to see the inside information about the buyer or the seller, should there be any effect on logical acquisition/ divestiture game plans. Of course, "logical" is the important word here.

Equity-Related Debt

Since we are identifying and removing speculation from our debt and equity financing decisions, let's take a look at a special, and more difficult problem, namely, *convertible debt*. We can issue debt that may turn into equity, such as a bond that converts into shares of common stock at a designated conversion ratio with an implicit designated conversion price.

As discussed in Chapter 18, our goal is to sell equity in the future at a higher price than the current market price of our stock. Well, what if we have the proverbial inside information? If we know the market is underestimating the upward potential of the stock, we must be careful to set the conversion price high enough to reflect that potential. Yet, since the market does not realize that this potential stock appreciation is realistic, we may find ourselves stuck with an interest rate on the bond that is higher than normal for a convertible issue. If this is the case, we may also wish to reconsider not issuing convertible bonds at all.

What if the reverse is true, and the market does not realize our stock is likely to rise slowly, but we know it? Then we must not be greedy in setting a high conversion price, or the debt may never convert to equity. Non-conversion is, paradoxically, the major risk of convertible bonds, as discussed in Chapter 18. Hopefully, we will still obtain a worthwhile benefit in terms of a low interest rate. Yet, once again we should reconsider whether a convertible issue is really the order of the day.

Summary and Conclusions

To sum up, speculation is not a dirty word, but it is also not a good idea because you really cannot beat the market consistently over time without inside information. While it is easy to spot your naive, unprofessional friends speculating in the stock market, it is a little more difficult to spot more subtle speculation, especially in the accepted practices of corporate financial managers. If we are such corporate financial managers, we are usually merely addressing the normal decisions related to financing the corporation. Should equity or debt be used? If the debt is used what should the maturity be, and should the rate be fixed or floating? And in what currency should any loan be denominated?

The key is always to second-guess ourselves. We must spot any predictions on stock prices, interest rates, and exchange rates that may be explicitly or implicitly incorporated in our decisions and that are not supported by inside information. Then we must remove such predictions as de facto speculation and make the decisions anew.

CHAPTER 13

Selection of Maturities
of Investments and Borrowing

We know we should avoid speculation, but we must select some maturities for investment of our excess cash and/or for borrowing funds needed for our business. So if we are not trying to beat the market by selecting maturities with more favorable interest rates, what criteria should be used in the selection process?

Matched-Maturities Rule

Maturities for investment should merely be matched with the duration of the funds to be invested. Seasonal or other temporary buildups of cash should be invested in marketable securities with maturities that match the expected time lag before the cash level declines. When the money must be used to finance seasonal account receivables, inventory, or net working capital requirements, or to finance a near-term planned capital spending program, it is advantageous to be able to liquidate the investment quickly. This is best handled by a natural maturity of the investment at the time the financing need occurs.

Otherwise, the next best choice would be liquid assets, with low transaction costs required for liquidation, plus little risk of loss on the principal from changing market conditions.

If longer-maturity, less-liquid assets were utilized, then you could find it difficult to obtain liquidity when needed without a loss. You might be left with a two-horned dilemma—one being the aforementioned loss of principal and the other being the need to borrow for your business while excess funds are tied up in securities. The latter situation increases total capital, probably reduces returns on capital, and increases the debt/capital ratio. In Chapter 21, we discuss the cost of such capital increases where we wind up earning a low money market return on capital with a high required return (say 30 percent pre-tax).

Of course, if a planned expansion program is far off, excess cash can be invested in either other projects within the business or other non-liquid investments. For example, stock market or real-estate investments for a few years may be satisfactory if the returns are significantly higher than marketable securities and the risk is considered acceptable. For such investments, the liquidation should be planned and begun well in advance of the spending requirements.

Perhaps a better strategy for longer-term investments of excess cash would be to repurchase stock during the period in which excess funds are no longer needed in the business. In a few years, when capital spending can utilize the funds, new equity can always be issued. Also, in many cases, retained earnings will have already rebuilt the cash level available.

An analogous approach should be applied to borrowing needs. Debt maturities should be selected that match the duration of the financing need. Seasonal and temporary needs, such as seasonal working capital and plant start-up expenses, should be funded by short-term commercial paper or indefinite-term bank lines/revolving credit. Longer-term investments in the business need to be funded by longer-term loans and bonds. Again, the goal is not to be borrowing money when there is no need for it, because doing so increases capital, reduces returns on capital, and increases the debt/capital ratio as we will discuss in Chapter 21.

Yet, some needs are "permanent" or of such a long-term nature that they can be treated that way. For example, if there is a debt/capital ratio target that will be maintained by capital spending or expansion programs or a stock repurchase program, and if the cash flows from operations are always positive and growing over time, then we must assume that all incremental debt will be maintained in the capital structure indefinitely. The matching maturities may then be infinite or at least the longest term available. In this situation, however, we should be flexible and redefine the matching-maturity period as the longest term that is *readily* available in the debt-market segments with the most favorable interest-rate structure. Thus, a ten-year Eurobond (in dollars or a given foreign currency) that saves 50 basis points on a foreign exchange-adjusted basis, compared with a ten-year bond in the U.S. market, could be quite suitable.

Exceptions to the Rule

Taking our new-found flexibility forward, even for definite-term financing needs, we should never look away from special opportunities for interest-rate savings, broadened exposure, convenience, and so on. If we have a preference for a given market segment, or that segment prefers our company over comparably rated firms, we should not forego consideration of such opportunities merely because the maturities do not match perfectly.

This is especially true for long-term maturities where all sorts of refinancing will likely be done. After all, as the economist Keynes once said, "We are all dead in the long run."

So, it would obviously be foolish to finance a new factory with 30-day commercial paper because the interest-rate savings are one percent or 100 basis points lower than a 30-year bond. We have experienced this type of debt financing in Latin America, where there is often little or no long-term debt available for corporations (either local or multinational) to finance their long-term requirements. Yet this would not be a good idea in the U.S., even for interim financing, unless these commercial paper rates were a bargain relative to other short-term rates; for example, in an inverted-yield curve situation when short-term rates are higher than long-term rates.

By the same token, it would be just as foolish to forego 100 basis-point savings because we could only obtain 12-year funds at a good rate and the projections called for a 15-year financing need. Along the same lines, it would be foolish to finance in either the U.S. or European market, when the other is more desirable for our overall financing plan, in order to merely obtain an exact maturity fit. The same would hold true if we had a preference for a public issue, compared with a private placement, or vice versa.

There is also another exception to the longest-matched-maturity approach, that is, varying the maturities for diversifying the interest-rate risk. Since the interest rate for any one maturity date may become very high relative to the changing market rate, there is a risk in having all of a corporation's debt mature on one date. Varying the maturities will give the company more and earlier opportunities to refinance. Also, if rates are suddenly high at a given maturity date, not all the debt need be refinanced at this undesirable point in time.

Interest Rates and Yield Curves

At the beginning of this discussion, we assumed that our criterion was not to beat the market and obtain favorable interest rates as compared with future trends. This was a continuation of the Chapter 12 caveats against speculation without true inside information. Let's explore more fully, however, the relationship between interest rates and maturities to see if we can better understand the specific rationale involved.

There are two basic explanations of the relationship between today's short-term and long-term interest rates. First, expectations for future short-term interest rates may be incorporated into long-term rates. In other words, long-term rates are merely the average of current and expected future short-term rates. For example, a three-year interest rate of ten percent would be:

Arithmetic average estimate:

$$10\% = (8\% + 10\% + 12\%)/3$$

Geometric average precise calculation:

$$9.988\% = (108\% \times 110\% \times 112\%)^{1/3} - 100\%$$

Second, liquidity preference by investors/lenders may cause the yield curve to slope upward, even when expectations for future short-term rates are flat. The *yield curve* is a line plotting interest rates on the vertical axis and maturities on the horizontal axis of a graph. In other words, there would be an additional cost for longer-term debt, apart from any projections on interest-rate trends.

Empirical evidence appears to support both explanations, with an emphasis on expectations. Now, if expectations of future interest-rate trends are the key to understanding long-term rates, how can you beat the market by selecting any maturity? If today's short-term rates are low for the borrower and long-term rates are high for the investor/lender, over time both parties will come out with the same result by going short or long in terms of maturities.

On the other hand, if liquidity preference is the key, you could always save interest expense and lose interest income by borrowing/ investing at lower rates for short-term maturities. Yet, the corporate borrower could view the additional average expense over time as an insurance premium or hedging cost which gives him the knowledge of his future interest expenses to use for financial planning and investment decisions. This investor/lender could view the loss of interest incomes as a tradeoff for the lack of transaction expense associated with the constant selling of unmatured long-term assets whenever liquidity is needed before maturity.

That brings us to the concept of riding the yield curve. The best example is the investor who borrows short term, invests long term, and either constantly refinances the short-term debt or sells the long-term assets to repay the debt. If liquidity preference and an upward sloping yield curve is the reality, then these tradeoffs must be evaluated.

Remember, however, the yield curve appears to be more a matter of expectations on future short-term interest-rate trends than liquidity preference. Thus, the constant refinancing at short-term rates could be very risky, unless you can forecast market trends better than the yield curve does. Savings banks, and to some extent, commercial banks, learned this lesson the hard way in the late 1970s and early 1980s.

Now what does this tell you about riding the yield curve or borrowing/investing on the basis of any viewpoint on the future interest-rate trends? Why, of course, it is speculative and risky. How can we avoid the problem? Why, of course, by matching maturities and focusing on duration, or by borrowing or investing cash as long as the need or resource is readily available. Any other approach could be a major financial mistake, and your de facto ride on the yield curve could become a ride on a most bumpy roller coaster.

Separate Financing Decisions from Working Capital Management

Before we close this topic, let's touch on one other related source of confusion. Even some of the best textbooks treat short-term debt as part of working capital management. As shown in Chapter 2, this simply is not a valid approach. Both short-term debt and long-term debt are funding sources for capital requirements, along with equity. All three types of funding carry interest costs or required returns that must be covered by the return of capital. Working capital, on the other hand, is merely one of the two broad components of capital, along with fixed assets, that is invested in a business to generate profit returns.

The correct approach is shown by the very definition of "net cash" at CBS. Net cash is viewed as the funds available to finance the working capital needs of inventory and receivables not already covered by interest-free payables. The bank cash balances considered available are reduced by bank debt and any other interest-bearing obligations, since they do place a burden on the operations.

Working capital management, therefore, seeks to minimize the amount of working capital by decreasing current assets or increasing non-interest-bearing liabilities within constraints of properly operating your marketing/productivity/distribution functions of the business. Thus, the selection of short-term debt is not even a decision possibility until working capital has been managed to produce some overall capital need to be funded by a combination of short-term debt, long-term debt, and equity.

Summary and Conclusions

The rule of maturity is to match the duration of the funds, either to be invested or to be borrowed, with the timing of the business needs for the funds. For investments, maturity is determined by the changes in the availability of current funds, the type of assets in which the funds are invested (liquid or non-liquid), the transaction costs required for liquidity, and the risk plus the return on the investment. For debt, maturity is determined by the duration of the current need for funds, the effect on the capital and its returns, and the debt/capital ratio. Therefore, the maturity should be planned and redefined, if necessary, in financial decisions, but speculation on future interest-rate trends should not be the key factor.

CHAPTER 14

Currency and Interest-Rate Swaps

Next to speculation, swapping has become perhaps the most pervasively misused strategy today. Many bankers and investment bankers treat swaps as a panacea for whatever ails you, such as the risk of high interest expenses, foreign currency exposures, or blocked funds. While there are certainly many constructive uses of swaps, and they do represent a natural adjunct to the globalization and linkages of many capital and currency markets, we must be very specific and selective in developing and implementing any swap strategy.

There are basically two types of swaps: currency/debt swaps and interest-rate swaps.

Currency/Debt Swap Purposes

Basically, only three purposes or situations call for consideration of these swap opportunities. Foreign currency swaps:

1. Can be used to obtain a low net effective interest rate on newly-issued debt;
2. Might allow repatriation of blocked funds; and

3. Can obviously allow the incurrence of debt in a currency to fulfill an exposure management strategy without requiring the issuance or retirement of actual debt.

Let's see how the currency/debt swaps can work in each of these cases.

Newly-Issued Debt

Many multinational companies have the choice of issuing in the U.S. or the European markets. They similarly have the choice of issuing debt in dollars or foreign currencies. Of course, if dollars are required to finance capital expenditure, the proceeds from any foreign currency debt can easily be converted. Yet, what if the firm is willing to take a new foreign exchange risk by leaving the debt denominated in foreign currency? Then, as is true for most American firms, the debt would either be covered in the long-term forward market or, even more likely, swapped back into dollar debt. The swap entails another company or financial institution taking over your debt obligations in return for your taking over designated interest and principal obligations denominated in U.S. dollars.

For example, we know of several investment banking firms that have become major players in the currency swap field by finding swaps that will make the all-in cost of foreign currency debt issue cheaper than U.S. or Eurodollar issues. Similarly, some competitive swap banks have been named as lead managers or co-lead managers on many debt issues as a result of their ability to provide favorable-term swaps.

Now, in perfect worldwide financial markets, neither the use of long-term forward contracts nor swap opportunities should allow the net interest rate in dollars to be lower than a straight issue of a dollar-denominated bond or note. Yet, in many situations, the market imperfections do yield net effective dollar rates that are more favorable. CBS, for example, has found many opportunities in several different markets at given times to obtain savings of at least 25 basis points, including the $50 million Eurosterling issue floated in late 1984.

Blocked Funds

Creative bankers and treasurers realize that swapping debt obligations can be combined with an initial exchange of currencies to give a U.S. company more dollars in the U.S. The structure is really one of parallel loans—giving up blocked funds abroad as a loan and taking dollars in the U.S. as a loan. If the two transactions are combined—with a right of set-off for any default, where the failure to pay interest or principal by one party excuses the obligation to pay by the other party—we have a swap.

Many banks have presented these swaps or parallel loans under various names as the answer to all major blocked-funds problems. Yet, as we will see below, the results do not usually fulfill the expectations.

Foreign Exchange Exposure Management

Currency/debt swaps can also be used to create a liability in a foreign currency to offset or hedge a net-asset position or any other long position for the term of the debt. Yet, if you prefer to hedge short-term foreign exchange exposure, such as payables and receivables, in a continuous use of forward-market contracts, then a swap may not be useful for this strategy. In fact, this is usually true. Also, if you do not feel there is a need to hedge net-asset positions, since their foreign exchange gains and losses are reflected only on the balance sheet and not on the income statement, then the swap would also not be used. Again, this is true of most American firms. Nevertheless, under the accounting principles set forth in FASB #52, there is a related benefit of a currency/debt swap that is gaining even more popularity today.

If you swap dollar debt into a currency with a lower interest rate and one in which you have a net-asset position, and if you designate the debt as a hedge, then all foreign exchange gains and losses on the principal can be hung on the balance sheet, as already stated. Even after interest obligations are covered by swaps or forward contracts, the net effect will still be a significantly lower interest expense on the income statement. We know of many corporate treasurers who have utilized this mechanism.

Requirements for Currency/Debt Swaps

Now let's review all the requirements and procedures for successfully using currency swaps to achieve each of these three purposes.

First, for a lower-cost debt issue with the dollar being the ultimate obligation, arbitrage opportunities are a must. If a foreign currency market has a particular demand for debt of our type of company, then this may provide the very comparative advantage upon which arbitrage is best based. For our company as the issuer, even though a foreign currency bond or note is issued and a swap is then used to get back dollars, the net effect is still merely a lower-cost dollar debt. Since bankers and investment bankers usually give package deals, there is no particular burden in going through a more complex structure—we merely wind up with a lower-cost dollar debt. We also need not worry about finding either the arbitrage opportunities or the markets when we have the same comparative advantages. The only concern is the package deal with lowest-cost dollar-debt interest from a banker or investment banker you trust.

The second purpose of currency swap, however, to repatriate blocked funds, is much more of a problem. A parallel loan really does not yield the desired effect. The dollars received in the U.S. are merely reflected as any new dollar loan, which is the same as you could get from any bank even without lending blocked funds abroad. The blocked funds are similarly reflected as a loan receivable, which is merely a different type of cash investment abroad. In other words, with a two-piece parallel loan structure, nothing really happens in terms of repatriation. In fact, if foreign operations are consolidated, the corporate capital level is actually increased. (See Chapter 21 for a more complete discussion of hidden capital.)

The only excuse to pursue such a strategy, therefore, is if for some reason the interest rate in one or both countries is favorable—and this is not usually true. CBS, for example, has reviewed several proposed deal structures for the ever-popular parallel loans of Greek drachma for U.S. dollars. The quoted interest rates on one or both sides were worse than the market rates from the CBS perspective; and, of course, defeasance could not be obtained.

Remember the combined loans with a right of set-off? Well, this would eliminate both the U.S. loan and the foreign loan receivable because of accounting rules on defeasance, resulting in de facto repatriation. Yet, if a country has blocked-currency repatriation, such a deal structure is almost positively illegal.

For the third purpose, currency swaps can again be quite effective. If you wish to increase liabilities in a given currency—especially to play the FASB #52 designated hedge game in a low-interest-rate currency in which you have a net-asset position—then you may not need any additional debt funds. Also, even if you did need funds, not all currencies offer good debt floatation opportunities for all companies or for all maturities. A swap, therefore, can be the cleanest way to play this particular game.

Figure 14-1 will clarify this somewhat complex procedure. The example shown in the figure is in three low-interest currencies. One of the authors has taken out $260 million of currency swaps (the first $60 million of which is shown in the diagram) in three low-interest currencies—Japanese yen, Swiss francs, and Dutch guilders. The interest savings shown on the income statement on the $60 million swap should be about 400 basis points over 5 years, even after covering the interest-payment exposures with forward contracts. The offsetting exposure on the principal, that would normally eat up this gain, is covered instead by significant net investments in these countries; these investments are designated as hedges. German marks are another common, low-interest currency for this game plan.

Figure 14-1. Currency/Debt Swap Structure

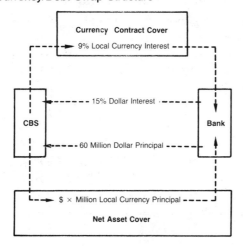

Interest-Rate Swaps

Now let's turn to the other type of swap—interest-rate swaps. This vehicle allows the switching of fixed-rate instruments to floating rates and vice versa. Naturally, if we decided to take or change a position on interest-rate trends and we had no need to borrow more funds at a given time, interest-rate swaps would be a perfect mechanism. We could swap floating rates for fixed rates when we thought interest rates would rise, and we could swap fixed rates for floating rates when we thought interest rates would fall. If your overall strategy does not include speculative practices, this game plan should not be used.

Yet, let's say that our ability to issue commercial paper or to obtain other short-term debt was better than the prospects for a long-term debt issue. Or let's say we prefer to avoid all the procedures accompanying a long-term public issue. We could still simulate the interest-rate certainty or fixed debt by swapping floating interest for fixed obligations. Then our short-term interest-rate obligations would be covered as we continuously reissued short-term debt, and our sole obligation would be to pay the fixed interest rates as if we had issued long-term debt on the front end.

Summary and Conclusions

We have discussed only three specific purposes or uses of both types of swaps that warrant consideration:

- *Situation 1: Currency/debt swap and foreign currency debt issue—* To achieve the lowest net dollar interest rates on a new debt, or, alternatively, to obtain better terms, such as earlier call provisions, use of zero coupons, and so on, without an increase in interest rates.
- *Situation 2: Currency/debt swap of existing debt*—To change or create the foreign exchange exposure for an economic hedge of net assets or to play the FASB #52 designated hedge game in low-interest-rate currencies in which you have a net-asset position.
- *Situation 3: Interest-rate swap from floating to fixed rates*—To lock in long-term rates without having to obtain long-term debt funds in a

more cumbersome manner or in a market where you feel your firm will be at a comparative disadvantage. For example, one aim could be to lock in rates over the long term for short-term commercial paper, rather than using a public issue of long-term bonds.

The basic mistake in this area is to look at the potential benefit of swaps as something different from the underlying purposes (as outlined). For each one of these purposes, a fundamental set of economic/market factors determines nearly all of the financial results. Also, for each of these purposes, several alternative mechanisms can fulfill the same need, and these alternatives are also governed by the same set of financial/ economic market factors. Thus, for all of the swap opportunities discussed as being worthy of consideration, we must still consider them as being merely one alternative means to reach a desired end.

Alternatives

Some of the basic alternatives for each of the three types of swap purposes are as follows:

● *Situation 1: To obtain the lowest dollar interest rates on new debt by means of a:*
—U.S. dollar market debt issue
—Eurodollar market debt issue
● *Situation 2: Incur foreign exchange liability to hedge net assets or to play FASB #52 game in low-interest currencies (where net-asset position exists) by means of a:*
—New debt issue in foreign currency
● *Situation 3: Lock in long-term interest rates by means of:*
—Long-term debt issues
—Long-term bank loans with fixed rates
—Interest-rate hedges
—Interest-rate collars and caps

We must therefore safeguard against being mesmerized by the "swapping panacea" by taking a three-step approach:

- First, designate the financial strategy and purpose for which a swap is being considered. If a swap is being proposed by a banker, then we should similarly first identify the purpose—or better yet, make the swap-seller/banker do it for us.
- Second, once we have zeroed in on the strategy and purpose, we must identify all the basic alternatives to a swap.
- Third, we must choose the best alternative on the basis of convenience (or the absence of restrictions) and the existence of arbitrage opportunities. The choice can be made simple, however, by merely shopping around among several bankers and investment bankers. By choosing the proposals with the lowest net costs, we automatically obtain the best arbitrage opportunities. By selecting the best overall terms and/or easiest procedures/deal structures, we provide the most convenience or cause the least restriction problems.

CHAPTER 15

Basic Interest Calculations

There are two esoteric mathematical concepts underlying interest-rate calculations. For you mathematicians practicing as financial analysts, they should be no problem. For the rest of you, please bear with us and perhaps this chapter will be of some use to you.

Basic Components of Capital Costs

What are the components of capital costs? Of course, they must be the costs of each type of debt and each type of equity, including the post-tax interest rate on bank loans, bonds, and the like, plus the return of preferred stock, common stock, and so on. Yet, each of these components has a similar set of fundamental elements—the elements upon which every interest rate on debt and required return on equity are based.

The following are basic elements of interest and return:

- *Riskless return*, which can be called a "pure return." In the U.S., we like to think of the return required and available on the U.S. Treasury debt as being reflective of such a rate.

- *Inflation rate*, which must be covered in addition to the real riskless return in order for the dollars received in the future to have the same purchasing power necessary to provide the desired/required real riskless return.

- *Risk premium*, which must be covered over and above the inflation return rate in order to satisfy the average risk-aversion desires of the average investor or lender of a given debt or equity instrument. There are also several subcomponents of risk to be considered:
  —*Debt business risk*, which will cause some default on debt instruments as a result of declines in earnings and cash flows below the fixed-charged coverage levels
  —*Debt political/economic risk*, which covers a myriad of additional default possibilities for foreign investments of a domestic or foreign borrower
  —*Equity risk*, which greatly increases the chances of lower-than-anticipated returns when the safeguards of fixed commitment debt are removed. In reality, this risk represents the increased amount of business and political/economic risk allowed to fall through to the investor not protected by debt-instrument safeguards.

Combining Capital-Cost Components

When all of these elements are incorporated into investor/lender thinking and market prices, the resultant rates will be the market-interest and required-return rates for various debtor and equity instruments available in the capital markets.

Does this then mean that we can merely add the inflation rate and risk premiums to the riskless rate? No, and you guessed it—this is the very financial mistake we are after. The elements of interest/return cannot be added any more than quarterly interest rates can be added together to obtain the compound annual rate. The elements must be *interactive*, which is mathematically equivalent to being compounded.

To make this point clear, the following are the two possibilities for a real return a, inflation rate b, and a risk premium c.

- *Incorrect additive approach:*
    Interest/Required return $= a + b + c$

- *Correct interactive approach:*
  Interest/Required return = $[(1+a) \times (1+b) \times (1+c)] - 1$

Let's look at some numerical examples. How about a nice low interest rate of 8 percent? It is stated to be composed of real return, inflation and risk premium requirements of 3 percent, 4 percent, and 1 percent, respectively, similar to the 1984 to 1985 period. Yet, if these were individual elements, then the effective interest rate would be slightly higher, at 8.2 percent, as follows:

$$(103\% \times 104\% \times 101\%) - 1 = 8.19\%$$

Alternatively, of course, each element could merely be slightly reduced, for example, to the 2.94 percent, 3.9 percent, and 0.98 percent levels, respectively.

Suppose we are in a period of higher interest rates, such as the 20 percent level of several years ago. Then the differences become a little more significant. For example, the elements of a 3 percent real return, 13 percent inflation rate, and 3 percent risk premium add up to only 19 percent, but could interact to produce nearly the full extra percentage point in interest levels required to reach 20 percent, as follows:

$$(103\% \times 113\% \times 103\%) - 1 = 19.9\%$$

Now, what if we are talking about the much higher returns on equity? For a 40 percent pre-tax return, which was certainly realistic for many companies during the early 1980s, the combination of 3 percent real return, 13 percent inflation, and 20 percent risk premium adds up to only 36 percent, but could still support the 40 percent level, as follows:

$$(103\% \times 113\% \times 120\%) - 1 = 39.7\%$$

Thus, when dealing with equity return requirements, risky interest rates, or local foreign currency interest rates in hyperinflationary countries, the interactive characteristics could add many percentage points to the resultant interest/return rates.

One of the elements of interest rates is used to a great extent by some financial analysts, both on "the Street" and in the corporate sphere. Risk premiums are part of the *capital asset pricing model* (CAPM). They are shown as being added to the riskless interest rates on U.S. Treasury debt to obtain required return on equity. They account for the risk of taking an equity position, as opposed to a creditor position, in a company with some business risk, in contrast to the "safest" organization in the world, which is the U.S. government (from the view of most U.S. investors). They are available for the whole stock market or any individual company, with the former being adjusted by each company's "beta" factor to obtain the latter. They can be used by security analysts to value stock, and by corporate treasury analysts to estimate the cost-of-equity component in the firm's cost of capital. Yet, please note that we referred to the risk premiums in the CAPM formula as being added to the riskless interest rate, not compounded with riskless rate.

Could the technical pros on "the Street" be wrong? Could there be a flaw in one of our basic financial models? Well, of course there could be, but we do not believe this is the case. The risk premium for the marketplace is not a separate element of the interest calculation, but rather a pragmatic representation of the answer. Once the "true" required return is established by the proper interaction of the risk premium and the riskless rate (which is itself based upon pure return requirements and inflation), then that answer is merely expressed in a simplified, addition form.

Similarly, when real interest rates are discussed in some of the periodicals, they may represent the subtraction of an inflation premium from U.S. Treasury rates. The correct calculation, of course, is to deflate the Treasury rates by dividing by one plus the inflation rate. Yet, the first form is a mere representation of the correct answer—an approximation rather than an actual calculation—and is quite accurate at low interest and inflation rates.

An analogous situation occurs in a more practical sense in one of the specific trading areas of the marketplace. Forward contract foreign exchange rates are often expressed in the form of the currency exchange rate (*spot rate*) *plus* or *minus* a premium or discount. That premium is supposed to offset the interest differentials between the currency being purchased or sold forward and the other currency being exchanged. (The underlying theory is that arbitrage will be prevented and the future exchange rates will be forecasted. The latter would be based upon the relationship between interest differentials, inflation differentials, and exchange-rate trends under interest-equilibrium and purchasing-power parity theories as presented in Chapter 11.) The interest-rate differentials, however, should be interactive and compounded to arrive at the net effect, namely, the interest rate in the other currency.

Once again, the answer is being calculated correctly by the marketplace in terms of "deflating/inflating" exchange rates with the proper compounding formula. Then, that answer is merely expressed as an addition/subtraction percentage to/from the current exchange rate—which is a much more practical form for the trading room.

Finally, we can cite one example from personal experience to demonstrate how important this esoteric concept can be. In estimating the interest-rate bids in a foreign currency, when the executive co-author swapped debt obligations in dollars (see Chapters 14 and 17), the following formula proved to be quite accurate:

$$\begin{matrix} \text{True} \\ \text{guilder rate} \\ \text{to be swapped} \end{matrix} = \left[\left(1 + \begin{matrix} \text{Dollar rate} \\ \text{to be} \\ \text{swapped} \end{matrix} \right) \Big/ \left(1 + \begin{matrix} \text{Dollar} \\ \text{market} \\ \text{rate} \end{matrix} \right) \times \left(1 + \begin{matrix} \text{Guilder} \\ \text{market} \\ \text{rate} \end{matrix} \right) \right] - 1$$

$$12.10 = (1.145/1.1088 \times 1.0855) - 1$$

The interest differential, therefore, was not arithmetic and was somewhat dependent upon the level of interest rates in general. In other words, the following formula was proven to be *incorrect*:

$$\begin{matrix} \text{Apparent} \\ \text{guilder rate} \\ \text{to be swapped} \end{matrix} = \begin{matrix} \text{Dollar rate} \\ \text{to be swapped} \end{matrix} - \begin{matrix} \text{Dollar} \\ \text{market rate} \end{matrix} + \begin{matrix} \text{Guilder} \\ \text{market rate} \end{matrix}$$

$$12.18\% = 14.5\% - 10.88\% + 8.55\%$$

Up-Front Costs and Interest Rates

All debt issues, premiums/discounts, and issuance costs can have a significant effect on the overall effective interest rates actually being paid by the issuer or borrower. Similarly, the up-front points paid to a bank for a home-mortgage loan can greatly affect the real interest rate being charged. When this concept is explained or taught, it is often stated that you merely divide the interest rate—the face rate or nominal rate adjusted for any less-than-annual compounding—by the percentage of the total debt actually received as net proceeds.

The simplest type of example is the one-year calculation where you receive 90 percent of a loan that has a 10 percent interest rate to be paid when the loan is repaid at the end of the year. An example is as follows:

$$\text{Apparent effective interest rate} = 10\%/90\% = 11\%$$

The proof that this calculation is incorrect is that $10 of interest will be paid for every $90 borrowed and received, and the $100 borrowed will be repaid for a total payment of $110 after one year. This results in a 22 percent interest rate, as follows:

$$\$20/\$90 = 22\%$$

The reason that the simpler approach will not work is that you are not merely reducing the amount actually borrowed (the net proceeds received) while holding the interest constant, but are also repaying more in principal than the amount actually borrowed. This excessive repayment of principal is equivalent to the repayment of additional interest. In our one-year example, the excessive repayment of principal amounted to $10, which is 11% of the net proceeds; this 11 percent must be added to the interest paid.

The correct formula for a one-year calculation, therefore, is:

$$\frac{\text{Effective}}{\text{interest rate}} = \frac{(\text{Interest rate} + \text{Discount\%} + \text{Fee\%} + \text{Expenses\%})}{(100\% - \text{Discount\%} - \text{Fee\%} - \text{Expenses\%})}$$

Not:

$$\frac{\text{Effective}}{\text{interest rate}} = \frac{\text{Interest rate}}{(100\% - \text{Discount\%} - \text{Fee\%} - \text{Expenses\%})}$$

If we have a multi-year maturity, however, such as in a bond or a home mortgage, there is no simple formula that works. You must account for each of the actual cash flows for each year. For a bond, this begins with the net proceeds received (after discounts, fees, and expenses) in year zero, and ends with the repayment of the full principal, which equals the gross proceeds (with the discounts, fees, and expenses added back) at the end of the last year. Interest is paid annually. For a home mortgage, the same receipts and payments are made, but the full principal is amortized over the life of the mortgage.

The reason that a simpler formula does not exist is that the extra interest, in the form of principal repayment greater than the net proceeds, is paid at different times in the future. Both the maturity term and the timing of the repayments in relation to the maturity can vary. The present value of this extra repayment, therefore, can vary significantly; thus, so does the all-in-cost/yield or effective interest rate.

In practice, we have seen some banker proposals that merely amortize the up-front costs over the life of the debt as an addition to interest. While this is often the correct accounting approach, the disregard of the time value of money could understate the all-in-cost (effective interest rate) significantly enough to distort a comparative analysis. For example, take an actual evaluation of Euro and U.S. debt issues:

Table 15-1. All-in-Costs (in $000)

	Euro	U.S.
Gross proceeds	$400,000	$400,000
Fees	10,000	4,000
Expenses	100	100
Net proceeds	$389,900	$395,900
Interest coupon rate	5.0%*	5.25%**
Maturity	15 years	15 years
Discounted annual all-in-cost	5.25%	5.40%
Amortized annual all-in-cost	5.17%	5.39%

*Annual basis. **Semi-annual basis.

Thus, the Euro rate advantage appears to be much greater (22 basis points rather than 15 basis points) when the up-front costs are amortized rather than present-valued in a discounted cash-flow calculation.

Average Balances and Interest Rates

Now, there is a situation where our first mistake will work quite nicely as an approximation. If there are no discounts or fees to consider, but the average loan balance outstanding is much less than the amount borrowed (due to principal repayments over time), the absolute amounts of interest paid should be reduced. Yet, in some situations, that amount will be calculated on the basis of the original principal amount, not the average balance. Such is the case with many auto loans, where the interest is expressed on an *add-on-basis*. Then the effective interest rate is probably double the level being shown, using the original formula of:

$$\text{Effective interest} = \frac{\text{Interest rate on original proceeds}}{\text{Net proceeds on average balance}}$$

$$= \quad 5\%/50\% = 10\%$$

For example, if the average balance is approximately one-half of the original loan amount—since the initial balance must be 100 percent and the final balance must be zero—then 5% added-on interest should be approximately 10 percent in terms of the effective rate.

Summary and Conclusions

While capital costs consist of the costs of each type of debt and each type of equity, there are also fundamental elements incorporated into it, which include:

- Riskless return;
- Inflation rate;
- Risk premium;
- Debt business risk;
- Debt political/economic risk; and
- Equity risk.

The calculation of the interest or return rate should be based on the interactive (compound) effect of these elements rather than an additive approach. The reason is that each element has an interactive effect on another. Similarly, this approach can be applied to determine interest-rate differentials in order to determine premiums/discounts on forward contract foreign exchange rates.

Some other interest calculations require modification based upon the type of payments, timing, maturity, and other terms. The most common examples are similar to up-front costs used by banks or average balances used by car dealers.

CHAPTER 16

Opportunity Costs and Required Returns for All Suppliers and Users of Funds

Turning away from the narrow, special topics of the last chapter, we will proceed directly to the other extreme. This discussion will cover the single most important issue in finance—what is the return on investments that should be required to cover the true cost of funds invested?

This concept is the pervasive cornerstone in all methods we have erected to allocate resources, or at least all those with a sound foundation. This concept is in fact the critical criterion to be satisfied to ensure that wealth is maximized. Interestingly enough, however, this is the very concept that also provides the link between all the perspectives of the various players with different stakes in the investment process, such as corporate managers, bankers, lenders, and shareholders/owners.

Unlike the last chapter, or some of the previous chapters, there is no one specific error to be addressed. The major mistake in this area is the failure to see just how broad the opportunity-cost/required-return concept really can be. Sometimes, pieces are merely overlooked. In other situations, the ''parts'' of our methodology are all handled properly, but are still not identified and understood as belonging to the same ''whole.'' So let's begin with the basic elements to show how the whole approach has been built and how the various parts fit into place.

Continuum of Opportunity Costs and Required Returns

The two basic elements of our extensive investment/allocation methodology are the concepts of opportunity cost and required return. Back in Chapter 2, we discussed the basic sources of funds invested in the firm and the cost of those funds. Obviously, the best source, or at least the cheapest, is the interest-free funds supplied by trade suppliers, employees, and so on. Some examples would be trade payables and accrued salaries. These are acceptable as long as they do not destroy the company's credit rating and are not counter-productive vis-à-vis their operating strategies.

Since these funds are interest free, they are included in the definition of capital. They merely reduce the amount of capital funds bearing a cost that are necessary to finance all the current and fixed asset requirements not financed by the interest-free funds. (We showed them as a reduction of current assets to obtain the relevant net working capital, which in turn was to be added to the fixed assets to obtain the total capital requirements.)

The other source, therefore, is the capital funds that, unfortunately, have a cost. These funds are debt proceeds, with a cost equal to post-tax interest expense and equity funds, with a cost equal to the required return by the shareholders. These equity funds are the retained earnings, or dividends foregone, and the proceeds from newly-issued stock. The weighted average of these debt and equity costs provides the cost of capital that must be covered before an investment becomes profitable enough to add value to the company. The latter will hopefully be reflected in the stock price.

Now, these capital costs represent the general, overall opportunity cost for any firm, because there is always the option of not spending the money on any project in the company. Then, either interest or dividends on new debt and stock will be saved, or existing debt and stock will be retired and repurchased, saving an equivalent amount of interest and dividends.

The company will also have specific opportunity costs within the firm every time one project is chosen to the exclusion of another. Such mutually exclusive projects, of course, should be ranked on the basis of maximum net present value discounted as the cost of capital, or on the incremental cash-flow internal rate of return (see Chapter 9).

The weighted average cost of capital also represents the returns required by the creditors and shareholders because they lend money to, and invest money in, the company based upon certain interest and dividend expectations. Even if the debt and stock were issued in the past, there are still current price fluctuations that bring the current yields back in line with the current interest and dividend expectations.

The cost of capital, therefore, can be viewed as representing the opportunity cost of investing in any of the projects within the firm, as opposed to returning the money to the creditors and shareholders to invest in loans and stocks of other companies. Since the other companies would use the proceeds for their own projects, the opportunity costs of investing in all external projects, which cannot possibly be reviewed by any one firm, are automatically accounted for. Yet, this involves merely the determination by the company that its own cost of capital is covered by the proceeds from its own projects, as long as they yield a positive net present value when the discount rate equals the cost of capital.

Therefore, we have only one, all-encompassing concept, i.e., the required returns by lenders and shareholders, specific opportunity costs of foregoing other projects, and the general opportunity costs of foregoing debt retirement, stock repurchase, and special dividends are all based on the ultimate return required. The actual return, therefore, must at least cover the required return, which is the same as being equal to or better than all the other opportunities for investment in the world that do not receive funding because as given projects within given companies, they do receive funding.

Complications of Different Tax Rates

One unnecessary complication of the above analysis is often raised. That is, the differences in investors' personal income tax rates. Yet, they have no meaning from either the corporate or the lender/shareholder perspective in terms of developing the appropriate opportunity cost/required return. The actual personal returns retained by the investors are not the issue, but rather, what are the returns that must be paid to the lenders and investors? These represent the opportunity cost of spending money in a company and foregoing the opportunity of retiring debt or repurchasing equity. These returns also represent the opportunity cost that will be applied by the marketplace to all other projects in all other companies, apart from risk adjustments.

The corporate income tax, of course, is an entirely different matter. The only funds that can be generated by any investment, from which to pay interest and dividends, are post-tax cash flows. Similarly, the net savings of cash by eliminating capital requirements and returning funds to creditors and shareholders is the post-tax interest and dividends.

We would view tax advantages or special deal structures for returning money to shareholders as potential exceptions to the rule. For example, in a stock repurchase, shareholders are given an opportunity to receive cash in return for tendering their shares at higher-than-market stock prices. Rather than paying ordinary income taxes on dividends—whatever their individual ordinary rates were—most of the shareholders would prefer capital gains treatment, with their cost-basis deducted.

While this lower tax for the recipients does not alter the money saved by the company on future dividends, it does represent an extra benefit to the tendering shareholders. Since most of the shareholders may tender, the post-tender ownership mix will remain fairly constant. The economic effect of the repurchase is, therefore, quite similar to a dividend to all holders, but the capital gains tax treatment increases the net returns retained after taxes.

Did our investors realize that a portion of their returns would always receive a favorable tax rate through a repurchase rather than through dividends? If so, there should be no effect on the cost-of-capital calculations used to derive our general opportunity costs for all investments in the company. If, on the other hand, the investors received an unexpected windfall, then the cost of capital relevant to the opportunity costs on the investment made in the company could be slightly overstated. This problem can be avoided by viewing each share as a separate investment that, once sold, should no longer be a concern of the company. Then the opportunity cost for the non-tendered shares is unaffected, but merely based upon future dividend prospects.

Apart from the tax considerations, and apart from corporate repurchases of stock, there is a general, related issue of shareholder sales to obtain capital gains. After all, isn't this the real mechanism to provide a shareholder with his required returns? Yet, as we discussed back in Chapter 2, resales of stock for capital gains are really no different from valuing the long-term dividend potential. Remember that capital gains on stock resales are a function of future dividend prospects under the dividend perpetuity model. Thus, any cost-of-equity calculation based upon dividend returns should still yield the same result as one based upon capital gains for the average shareholder over the long run.

Adjusting for Different Risk Levels

Now, there is one last point required to bring this perfect opportunity-cost concept back to the real world. Projects as well as companies vary in terms of risk. (See Chapter 15 for a discussion of business and financial risk, and see Chapter 11 for a discussion of international risk.) The company's risk variations are automatically accounted for by the creditors' and shareholders' preferences for risk aversion, thus yielding lower interest rates and higher stock prices. For individual projects that vary in risk levels both above and below the average, the firm's cost of capital must be adjusted to serve as the proper benchmark. When this is done, the adjusted cost of capital can provide a realistic, practical opportunity cost.

This real-world, risk-adjusted benchmark will then become all-encompassing. It can be used to represent both the company and creditor/shareholder perspectives and to account for all individual projects in both a given company and all companies.

Summary and Conclusions

As mentioned in Chapter 2, the weighted average cost of capital, which is the weighted average of the costs of debt and equity funds supplied to the corporation, is the opportunity cost if the funds are kept idle as excess cash. The cost of capital also can be the opportunity cost when the company chooses to invest in a project instead of returning money to the shareholders. The reverse also holds true, so that the cost of capital represents the opportunity cost of the company's investment in retiring debt and repurchasing equity.

These opportunity costs for the company also represent the required return for creditors and shareholders. In addition, they represent the opportunity cost of not investing in all the other projects outside the corporation, whether by the shareholders and creditors themselves, or by other corporations.

Differences in personal tax rates are already factored into the above. The investors set their required returns after making an assumption on the amount they will retain from dividend and interest received once they pay taxes. Yet, the company may take advantage of repurchasing stock in order to avoid shareholders paying tax on 100 percent of payments made to them as dividends. In this case, the tendering shareholders receive capital gains, and the opportunity cost for non-tendered shares is unaffected.

CHAPTER 17

Uses of Foreign Currency Debt

There are obviously many purposes for obtaining debt or any type of liability in a foreign currency. In practice, they can appear quite strange to basic financial analysis. Yet, there is one whole group of purposes that are similar to the strategies discussed in connection with currency/debt swaps in Chapter 14. Then, there is a second whole group that is related to all the operating needs of reducing exchange exposure created in connection with running a company's foreign operations.

There are also basically only two types of financial mistakes made in this area. First, we must learn to avoid implicit speculation on the foreign exchange-rate trends that pervasively pop up, as was generally discussed in Chapter 12 and more specifically addressed (with respect to swaps) in Chapter 14. Second, we must define all the purposes and alternatives quite specifically, in a manner similar to that of Chapter 14, to avoid the many panaceas touted. Some common solutions, such as currency/debt swaps, may really do nothing for you in handling the problems that concern your company in a given situation.

Reminder: Avoid Speculation

As you may remember, taking or changing any positions on currencies, based upon your outlook for foreign exchange rates, is speculation. Attempting to beat the market, rather than merely using the forward market to offset exposure, is speculation. Your goal is merely to break even by defining all exposures you have and by offsetting them with forward-market contracts whenever possible.

Foreign Currency Debt: A Handy Tool for Corporate Use

As you may also remember, the following are the only basic purposes for and alternatives to foreign debt for the overall corporation:

- *Foreign currency debt issue and currency debt/swap:*
  —It is used to achieve the lowest net dollar interest rates on a new debt.
  —Alternatively, it is used to obtain better terms, such as earlier call provisions, the use of zero coupons, and so forth, without an increase in interest rates.
  —It is based upon favorable borrowing conditions in one market versus another, for one company or for all borrowers in the given market.
  —By definition, it is an example of comparative advantage and/or arbitrage.
- *Foreign currency debt issue with liability retained in that currency:*
  —It is used to change or create the foreign exchange exposure for an economic hedge of net assets or to play the FASB #52 designated hedge game in low-interest-rate currencies in which you have a net-asset position.

With respect to the second item, let's take a look at the various elements of the FASB #52 game plan, which are illustrated in the diagram in Figure 17-1.

As you can see, without a net-asset position in a given currency, the foreign currency interest rate would be equal to the Eurodollar rate of 11.5 percent. The cost of covering the foreign exchange exposure on the principal and interest obligations with forward contracts would offset the 3.5 percent savings from the low foreign currency interest rate of only 8 percent. Yet, with the principal covered by the net assets being

Figure 17-1. Foreign Currency Debt

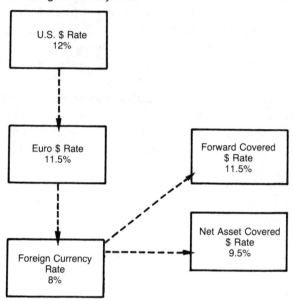

designated as a hedge, the amount of forward contracts required to neutralize the exposure is less, at only 1.5 percent, for a net savings of 2 percent or a full 200 basis points—that is, an interest rate of 9.5 percent as compared with the Eurodollar rate of 11.5 percent.

Could we save more by not using forward contracts, and could we save the full 3.5 percent even without a net-asset designated hedge? Why sure, if the foreign exchange rates do not increase the dollar value of the foreign currency principal and interest obligations. Yet, since the forward-market rates represent the market consensus about forecasted foreign exchange rates, this would be de facto speculation, as explained in Chapter 12.

Could we still save something by borrowing in a foreign currency versus borrowing in Eurodollars without speculating exchange rates? How about borrowing in Eurodollars versus borrowing dollars in the U.S. market? Well, in answer to the first question, the diagram does not show any arbitrage opportunities to borrow more favorably in foreign currencies, but as stated above, and as discussed in Chapter 14, a combined foreign currency debt/swap deal structure often provides some small savings attributable to arbitrage opportunities in a given market and/or for a given borrower. In answer to the second question, arbitrage savings of one-half percent or 50 basis points for the Eurodollar versus the U.S. market are shown in the diagram itself. For companies with good international reputations, such opportunities often exist.

At CBS, the executive co-author implemented the game plan outlined in the diagram with our $50 million Euro-sterling bond issue, though with smaller percentage savings. We found that borrowing in the European markets was cheaper for us at the time of bond issue. We then had enough net assets in sterling to act as a designated hedge for about half of the 40 million pound principal exposure. The remainder of the principal and interest obligations was covered with formal contracts, leaving us with a tidy net savings of approximately 100 basis points versus U.S. borrowing. And it was still safe and non-speculative!

As you can see from the above discussion, the use of foreign debt is very similar to the use of most currency/debt swaps seeking either arbitrage savings or a FASB #52 designated hedge game plan. The major difference, of course, is the existence of both of the following needs:

- To obtain new debt funds; and
- To leave debt in a foreign currency.

But a swap will either create a foreign currency obligation without new funds or eliminate a foreign currency obligation when new funds are borrowed in a foreign currency debt issue.

Foreign Currency Debt for Foreign Currency Operations

Some of the purposes cited above deal with the needs of the local foreign operations. The most obvious, of course, is merely the need to borrow local foreign currencies in order to run your operations in that country whenever you do not wish to make an equity contribution. (See the discussion of foreign subsidiary capital structures in Chapter 22.)

You probably need to borrow in the local currency in which you have net assets in order to avoid creating additional foreign exchange exposure attributable to the invested proceeds obtained from the new debt. You could always have your local subsidiary borrow in another currency—let's say a dollar-denominated loan obtained in the U.S. on behalf of the foreign subsidiary—and then convert the proceeds to local currency via the foreign exchange spot market. Yet, there would then be an increase in the net-balance amount of assets over liabilities in the local currency.

Another strategy to control the foreign operation exchange exposure is related to trade debt that is billed in the local foreign currency in which the revenues and profits are generated. Even before goods are received and resold, there can be movements of foreign exchange rates. Any local currency cost increases that result from billing in non-local currency may or may not be passed on in the form of local currency price increases as indicated under the *purchasing-power parity theory*.

This theory works quite well in the long run, but may have no practical relevance in the short run. After the goods are resold and accounts receivable are created in local currency, any payables that still exist in non-local currency may no longer be covered, and an operating profit can turn into a net loss. The easiest way to safeguard automatically and fully against such exposure is to be billed in local foreign currency, rather than any non-local currency, including dollars, even when there is a U.S.-based parent corporation.

Of course, not all suppliers are willing to change their billing practices. Also, some governments will not even allow such changes. The negotiations may also require a higher price for supplies, which must be weighted against the cost of covering non-local currency exposures in the forward market.

In Europe, one partial means of handling this billing among the many Common Market suppliers is to denominate invoices in *European currency units* or ECUs. The fluctuations of local exchange rates against ECUs are usually less. If a pure hedge policy exists, however, the residual exposure of each currency versus ECUs must still be covered with forward contracts.

Another means of neutralizing exposure for the individual foreign subsidiaries is to utilize a reinvoice center. This center, run by the parent corporation, can rebill all invoices to the subsidiaries in their own local currency. The overall exposure, of course, cannot be changed, but they can all be captured in one place in the reinvoice center. Nevertheless, this mechanism is really nothing more than a system of netting all the foreign exchange exposures.

A classic netting system merely reflects all foreign exchange exposures in two parts—the long and the short positions, or the positions where one foreign currency must be sold and the other one must be bought in the future. The reinvoicing center would merely add one preliminary step of transferring all the exposure to itself for all the local currencies and dollars. Then the center would become responsible for the exposure data on any item reinvoiced and for all the related accounting reporting of foreign exchange gains and losses that appear on a separate line on the income statement.

Let's take an example of an American company with operations in England and France. The English operations purchase $1 million worth of goods from suppliers in the U.S. and $1 million worth of goods from suppliers in France. The French operations purchase $2 million worth of goods from suppliers in England. The foreign exchange exposure, therefore, can be summarized as follows:

Table 17-1. Long/Short Positions

	Dollars (000)	Sterling (000)	Francs (000)
English operations			
• U.S. suppliers	($1,000)	$1,000	
• French suppliers		1,000	($1,000)
Subtotal	($1,000)	$2,000	($1,000)
French operations			
• English suppliers		($2,000)	$2,000
Total company	($1,000)	$ -0-	$1,000

The only net exposure that results in a $1 million long position in francs against a $1 million short position in U.S. dollars. Under a netting system, these would be the only exposures covered with forward foreign exchange contracts.

If we get fancy, in addition to foreign exchange contracts to hedge the net exposure at the reinvoice center, the payment schedules can be led or lagged. This would allow the net balances in one currency or another to be decreased so as to reduce the position that must be covered by the foreign exchange contracts. Of course, leading and lagging could also easily be used to establish greater or lesser positions in the currencies of your choice, namely, de facto speculation.

Restatement of the Problem

Beyond these somewhat limited purposes for foreign currency debt, there is no magic to international debt financing in foreign currencies. Thousands of variations in the structure of debt instruments, prevailing economic conditions, fundamental economic cause-and-effect explanations, and sophisticated titles for the basic strategies will all be used by the bankers in selling their services. Yet, the practical uses are relatively basic and few in number, as outlined above. Again, failure to see this relative simplicity and the failure to keep from being drawn into de facto speculation are two types of financial mistakes that are most common in the very broad areas we have discussed, namely, international debt markets, domestic and international interest-rate and currency swap markets, and currency-of-billing decisions.

Summary and Conclusions

Basically, foreign currency debt has limited purposes, since we try to avoid speculation. Foreign currency debt can be used as an alternative to provide lower interest expense. It can also be used to avoid or reduce transaction exposure, in lieu of forward contracts, especially in currency-of-billing decisions.

CHAPTER 18

The Benefits and Risks
of Convertible Securities

We all know what the apparent risks are with convertible securities, such as converting bonds into common stock at a premium price (either absolute or per some sliding scale). When the stock price jumps above the conversion price and the bondholder converts, he gets the benefit of a bargain, compared with the then current market price. Must this bargain then be considered our loss, as the issuing corporation that gambled on lower stock prices and lost? Is this not the real risk of issuing convertible debentures? Well actually, no! This mistake in ascertaining the real risk is the very financial problem we will discuss in this chapter.

Hybrid Benefits

There are basically two alternatives to issuing a convertible bond. First, we could always issue straight debt without a conversion option. Yet, the interest rate we then pay would always be higher. After all, the conversion option must be worth something to the bondholder. So, we could always issue non-convertible debt, but at a higher cost.

The second alternative is to issue equity right away at the current stock price. But if we issue stock now at the current price, and a convertible security's conversion price always incorporates some premium, the price to the new shareholder is lower and our cost of equity must be higher. So we could always issue stock now, but at a lower price.

Real Risk

If a convertible security is always cheaper to issue than either the straight-debt or current stock alternatives, why is there any risk? Well, what if the security never converts? Without conversion, you are left with another bond in your debt/capital ratio calculation. At the same time, your fully-diluted earnings per share—the ones the sophisticated security analysts focus on—are reduced. You have thus established the worst of both the debt and equity worlds, and not until conversion occurs, the term expires, or the securities are called or repurchased, does this problem go away. Obviously, therefore, the risk with a convertible security must be the potential lack of conversion.

Conversion Price Setting

In terms of price setting, does this mean that the highest conversion premium may not be best? On the front end, the higher the premium, the more difficult it will be to sell the convertible instrument itself at a given interest rate. More importantly, the real benefit of the convertible security—the combination of low-cost debt now and lower-cost-of-equity stock in the long run—cannot be obtained without conversion, which requires a conversion price that is likely to be exceeded over the planning horizon.

We all know that setting a bond coupon too low or a stock price too high greatly impedes a successful offering. Similarly, setting a conversion premium too high not only has the same negative effect on the issue, but will also impede the ultimate success of the whole game plan.

Corporate Value Effect

Assuming a convertible-debt issue is successful and a lower-cost debt is obtained now, with higher-priced stock being sold in the future as a contingent possibility, should we expect an immediate jump in the stock price? After all, we will just have reduced our current cost of debt and potential cost of equity. Yet, it is unclear if there will be any significant impact felt, at least if the company already had an optimal degree of leverage. (The benefits of more leverage, as cited in Chapter 20, will already have been obtained.)

We can look at this situation in several ways. First, on the negative side, while the cost of debt is lower, the convertible is also partially a higher-cost equity instrument. It can, therefore, be viewed as adding an equity cost to the capital-cost mix without immediately adding the usual increase in debt capacity. All this takes place at a lower-than-average equity cost that is attributed to the conversion price being higher than the current price of the stock. Since the cost of capital is a weighted average of the debt and equity components, this particular addition to the capital structure has less immediate impact than would other forms of lower-cost debt.

Let's take a more basic, but still negative approach. There is some possibility of non-conversion and some time-value-of-money discount. They must both be applied to future stock sale proceeds (from conversion), and they could combine to offset the impact of a higher conversion price on the long-term cost of equity.

On the positive side, in a particularly good situation, a convertible security can add value to the firm at the outset, just as any particularly good or creative use of the capital markets can. An issuer can beat the debt/equity combination market by merely combining a debt and equity instrument into one. The potential conflict with the efficient market hypothesis (the subject of Chapter 12) can be overcome by the service provided to the investor/lender. Perhaps this argument is most easily illustrated by drawing a simplified analogy to the insurance business.

The benefit to the issuer of the 'low-cost debt now and low-cost equity later' theory could be quite real, and this benefit could be viewed as his profit or premiums from the insurance business. Who is being insured? Why, the investor, of course, who is an extreme risk averter afraid of taking equity risks, but who still desires some of that potential to earn higher equity returns than the low-interest income levels. By providing such an investor a safe floor for his equity fling, after removing the ceiling that kept him from any equity returns, we have given him a valuable insurance policy. This policy is also wrapped up in one efficient package, so the investor need not set up a whole series of investments in debt securities, options, warrants, and such. After all, is this not what an insurance company does—provide an efficient service to make a profit?

If you feel this requires a degree of imperfection in the overall capital markets, we would agree. But what are such imperfections called? They are arbitrage opportunities that do exist in efficient, albeit imperfect, markets. *Arbitrage opportunities*, in general, are also a function of a particular comparative advantage of one company in a given market that offers the investor in that market something he desires, and cannot obtain without going to some other market where he feels less comfortable. Well, isn't that what we, and all insurance companies, really are doing? We are giving the investor/lender what he wants—an equity opportunity and a debt safety net, without requiring him to go beyond one market, or even beyond one security.

Corporate Financing Strategies

Now, back to the main theme of the benefits and roles of convertible securities for the issuer. Even if there is a risk in the convertible top being up for some time, there are two scenarios that a convertible would fit perfectly. We may need more debt now, either to reach an optimal capital structure with higher leverage or because inside information about our business prospects may tell us that this is the wrong time to sell stock. (See Chapters 20 and 12, respectively.) We may then need more equity in the future, either as part of a future expansion plan, requiring both debt and equity capital, or when the inside information on business prospects yield their results. For either set of circumstances, the benefits of a convertible are obvious and the risks will not be a burden in the long run.

Conversion will come when you need the equity, and you will make a profit when you sell it at the higher conversion-premium price. In the meantime, you have borrowed at a lower-than-market interest rate. Of course, this all assumes you are totally correct in forecasting the future results. Otherwise, you could lose from debt ratios remaining too high, while fully-diluted *earnings per share* (EPS) also bear the burden as if all the equity had been sold.

We touched on the conversion-premium price setting and inside information before. An interesting problem may arise when we combine these two phenomena. The business prospects known to management may be excellent, but may not yet be reflected in the market's evaluation of the stock price. The stock price should obviously rise more in the future than the market could expect. The conversion premium, therefore, can be high without adding undue risk of non-conversion. Yet, you must sit there and take a higher-than-market interest rate for a convertible security (less of an interest-rate reduction), since the premium appears too high; it may be difficult for most companies to feel comfortable with this strategy. Yet, your rewards will be obtaining reasonable-cost debt now and a more realistic price for your equity funding in the long run, as your inside knowledge is borne out by the future results.

When, in 1987, CBS issued the largest convertible debt in the history of the European market, all of these considerations were fully discussed. Later, the corporate planning model incorporated them and addressed their effects. Yet, the weights and probabilities given to each of the pros and cons were obviously different for each member of the management team involved in this necessarily subjective analysis.

What if this rapid stock appreciation potential, however, is deemed to be merely a function of a risky company in trouble? What if the mere issuance of a convertible security still bears a connotation of a company facing bankruptcy? Well, the stigma of issuing convertible securities appears to have passed in the U.S., and the European markets have accepted this type of issue from top-ranked companies all along. The latter, in fact, is just another example of arbitrage opportunities derived from comparative advantages of a given market, for a given company in that market, or for a given type of security.

High-Escalating Conversion Premium

Let's move on to a new convertible instrument that challenges the hypothesis of non-conversion being the big risk involved in convertible securities. Something called a LYON (liquid yield option note) was issued for a high-flying company, Waste Management. The conversion premium itself rapidly escalated over time according to a sliding scale. In addition, another anti-conversion incentive was utilized, since the note had a zero coupon, which usually means that all interest would be accrued until maturity rather than paid periodically; for this convertible, it also called for forfeiture of some accrued interest upon conversion. In other words, not only will the investors be charged rapidly increasing prices for the stock, but they will be penalized if they ever try to buy it.

The consensus on "the Street" appeared to be that conversion was unlikely. Yet, the company obtained a nice interest reduction. In other words, in economic terms, it could be an example of getting something (in the form of reduced interest cost) while giving up nothing (in the form of real equity dilution or the reasonable change of selling stock at a lower-than-future market price).

How about the marketplace, however, and the emphasis many security analysts place on fully-diluted earnings per share? Perhaps they would include a low probability factor in their analysis and emphasize only the primary EPS that would also be reported. In other words, the LYON could be viewed more as a sale of debt at a low interest rate, rather than as a future sale of equity at a higher price.

For an extreme case, with little likelihood of conversion from the outset, this approach may work. Yet, such situations will become harder to sell to the investors in the future. In order for the investors to become interested in this type of security, it is usually required that conversion still be a significant enough possibility and that fully-diluted EPS be a factor. Of course, if probabilistic, fully-diluted EPS were reported, this would solve our problem. But such calculations just are not in the auditor's repertoire under generally accepted accounting principles.

There is one specific benefit, however, from high-premium convertible debt. If conversion is unlikely based upon business as usual, but would become likely if a friendly acquisition takeover occurred, then this could be a form of a "poison pill" or anti-takeover defense. While the company would have the same fully-diluted EPS problem, it might be totally discounted by the marketplace except for their takeover speculation valuation. Since the company's current management may not be concerned with stock prices and EPS after a takeover, perhaps they would view the contingent convertibility as being solely the raider's problem.

Other Equity-Related Debts

There are several related types of instruments that should at least be mentioned in this chapter. *Convertible preferred* stock is less of a rainy-day problem because the initial form already represents equity for credits analysis and rating agency purposes. Yet, there is a dark cloud behind this silver lining; preferred dividends are both higher and non-tax-deductible. Thus, this instrument does not give you the low-interest debt to reduce your cost of capital, and the latter will increase, unless your debt leverage, exclusive of preferred stock, remains nearly as high as the original target.

Equity warrants are more similar to the debt securities convertible into common stock. Yet, *debt warrants* (the option to buy more debt in the future at the investor's choice) are completely different. They do represent a source of low-cost debt that will always remain debt. Their true risk, in fact, is that the company may be forced to have more debt and total capital outstanding than their future financing plans call for.

Summary and Conclusions

The combination of high leverage and fully-diluted EPS could cause a real problem if convertible debt does not convert. Some extremely high conversion-premium cases may be exceptions if fully-diluted EPS become unimportant. Yet, the true exceptions are few and far between, given the lack of probabilities being incorporated into the reported data.

Yet, it is true there may be some good arbitrage benefits for the issuer. It is also true that a future sale of equity after a current sale of debt may be a perfect fit into the financial plans and profit expectations of some companies.

CHAPTER 19

Hybrid Debt/Equity Securities

Hybrid Perceptions Vary with Purpose

Financial concepts change their nature as the perspectives of the parties change. Yet, in describing the nature of some financing instruments or financial securities, we may overlook this type of phenomenon. This leads to a mistake in the sense that we are seeking a definitive answer that cannot exist. All answers must change when we change who is asking the question or under what circumstances the question is being asked.

Preferred Stock

Perhaps, *preferred stock* is the best example. Is preferred stock debt or equity? As a corporate issuer of preferred stock, do we treat it as an alternative to debt financing or as a means of infusing new equity into the company? Obviously, these are both elements in our feelings, but which is the stronger one?

For the investor/lenders, preferred stock adds equity with respect to the debt/equity ratios concerning rating agencies and creditors. This is because preferred stock does give the creditors a cushion in terms of asset proceeds available to service the principal and preferred-dividend payments (both for an ongoing business or upon liquidation of the company). There is still some risk of delayed payments, however, since preferred dividends are not a fixed obligation if earnings are not generated—unlike interest payments.

For the common shareholders, preferred stock adds a fixed charge to reduce earnings available to them, which is the real definition of earnings per share (per common share). Yet, this charge is *not* totally fixed to the extent earnings are not generated and common dividends are not paid. From the Internal Revenue Service's point of view, *preferred stock is equity*. The preferred dividends, of course, are not tax deductible.

From the corporate issuer's perspective, therefore, *preferred stock is debt*, in terms of long-term EPS and ownership dilution. Yet, it does yield some of the benefits of equity—primarily in the form of a lower debt/equity ratio and, secondarily, in the form of more flexibility during periods where no earnings are generated. This beneficial type of *debt*, therefore, should have a higher cost in terms of yield—and it usually does. The much bigger addition to the cost, of course, is the loss of the tax shield.

In other words, this financing security changes its "colors," depending upon the circumstances, or more precisely, depending upon the viewer's perspective.

The basic tradeoff for this debt-type security is the improved debt/equity ratio in return for the loss of the tax shield. We feel the latter—which is totally a real economic burden amounting to approximately a two-thirds increase in the after-tax cost of this debt—outweighs the benefits of the lower debt/capital ratio for most companies. When a firm is at or above its debt/capital target, however, with little near-term relief in sight, then it certainly warrants serious consideration. In other words, it may be a nice touch to round out the overall capital structure, but only at a selected point in time for small amounts of the capital financing requirements and as a last resort to avoiding more debt.

There is one form of preferred stock that is a little less costly— *redeemable preferred stock* with a definite term. This qualifies it for the 80 percent intercorporate dividend tax exclusion rule. CBS issued more than $100 million of such ten-year stock at a yield nearly 100 basis points below that of the ten-year debt because of the tax benefits to the investor. The yields are commonly between that of a tax-free municipal bond and a corporate bond—because the slightly lower security for dividends and principal, compared with corporate debt interest and principal, is more than offset by the tax savings for corporate investors who determine the market price. The after-tax cost to the corporation, however, is still nearly twice that of the debt.

Convertible Debt

Let's review another type of security that we just discussed in the last chapter, namely, that of *convertible-debt securities*. How do they fit into our approach, and how do they compare with preferred stock?

As we discussed, most convertible debt should be treated by the corporation as a lower-cost form of equity financing being issued at a higher price, and thus with lower dilution in the future. While they are booked as debt until conversion, since the greater risk is non-conversion, we must always assume the corporation's game plan is to issue equity. Also, it would be too costly in terms of the fully-diluted EPS impact to be considered as a viable debt instrument.

This same equity-designation perspective should also hold for the common shareholder. After all, it is their earnings being diluted in the future.

For the creditors or rating agencies, however, convertible securities still represent either debt or an equity/insurance combination. The floor with respect to the return represents either the debt return or return on insurance policy. The reduction in interest rates represents the premiums, some of which can be the profits of the "insurance company," namely, the issuer.

Lease Financing

In Chapter 21, we will discuss *leases* as usually being treated as a form of debt financing and as part of the real capital structure. For the corporation, however, the nature of a lease also changes into more of a hybrid. Even if no risk is transferred to the lessor, the balance sheet treatment may be one of the sale of the asset without the loss of its use.

For the lessor, unless he is assuming the business risk for lower operating results and/or a reduction in the liquidation value, he will regard the transaction as financing. He borrows money and passes it on to the lessee at a higher internal rate of return than most loans will yield. Even if he assumes liquidation-value risk, it may be small for many types of assets being leased—such as real estate, rather than a computer, as discussed in Chapter 4.

International Loans

Other examples from Chapter 21, which we also have seen in Chapter 14, are parallel loans; funds are borrowed from a bank in one country and excess funds are deposited at a bank in another country. For the corporation that properly views its consolidated balance sheet as the key to the transaction, nothing really happens. Local deposit or borrowing rates may change, as compared with opportunity costs, but the loans and deposits themselves merely shift from one bank to another.

For the bank, however, they increase their primary business. More deposits are brought in and then loaned at a profit to a credit line customer. This increases the bank's overall deposit and loan levels at an average interest-rate spread in the bank's favor, which is certainly their primary, traditional business.

Another example can be drawn from *foreign subsidiary capital planning*, as we will discuss in Chapter 22. As we will see, the choice between foreign debt and equity capital at the foreign subsidiary level is really not a capital structure decision, in the normal financial sense, for the corporate staffs of many companies. Only if the goal is to set up autonomous subsidiaries, with stand-alone balance sheets and debt capacities, do we utilize the normal capital structure criteria. Otherwise, we are merely talking about management incentives, repatriation capacity, legal/tax implications, and consolidated balance sheet goals/ strategies when the capital structures of foreign subsidiaries are determined.

For the local management, however, as well as the foreign government and foreign banks, the local balance sheet and business entity may be all that they see or about which they care If so, it is a true capital structure upon which their evaluation is made; they may not understand the method to our madness from our consolidated parent perspective.

A related issue is one of foreign subsidiary taxes. High local tax rates for "excess" dividends or many other actions may appear to be a tremendous burden to the local management. If foreign tax credits are available, however, at the U.S.-parent level, we are merely talking about a timing difference. The high tax payments today will be offset at the very next corporate tax payment, and the only financial impact is the loss of interest at a cost of debt, or really a loss of time value at a cost-of-capital level.

Back in Chapter 14, we also discussed the real game plan utilized by many companies, including my own, with respect to designated foreign exchange hedges of net-asset positions under FASB #52. While the economists talk about using a loan to hedge that value, the real game plan is often merely to reduce the interest expense that hits the income statement and hang up any offsetting foreign exchange losses in the principal on the balance sheet. Remember, low interest-rate currencies generated lower interest expenses being booked, and the implicit increase on the principal obligation is charged to the *special equity* section of the balance sheet.

Summary and Conclusions

There are probably an infinite number of examples where the nature of given financial instruments changes with the perspectives of the parties involved. We have discussed preferred stock, convertible debt, lease financing, and various types of international loans in this chapter. Some of the changes in perception may be minor. Yet, it is often difficult to understand the real nature of the financial instrument or strategy involved until you track its chameleon-like changes over the complete spectrum of colors—which are its various uses and perceptions among the players and markets in the world of finance.

PART III

DEBT AND DIVIDEND LEVELS

CHAPTER 20

Acceptance of Higher Debt

We have all heard Benjamin Franklin's advice, "neither a borrower nor a lender be." Well, quite frankly, that is no longer a common misunderstanding of finance because few business professionals still follow it. But, we should begin our discussion of debt levels with at least a little background on why leverage can be beneficial.

Debt is obviously a great idea for the lender. After all, where would banks be if no one took out loans? They would be both safe and out of business.

Yet, for the borrower, the need for debt is nearly as obvious. With interest rates in the 10 percent range—usually only about 5 percent after the corporate income tax deduction—and required equity returns in the 15 to 20 percent range, there is an obvious favorable effect on capital costs from the substitution of debt for equity in the pool of capital funds. There is a limit, however, to the percentage of debt that can be utilized before both the interest costs and required equity returns increase as a result of the added risk associated with the added debt. When the substitution effect can no longer offset the increase in interest rates and required equity returns, then the lowest combined, overall capital cost has been reached. In other words, the borrower has attained the optimal capital structure or the highest debt levels that should be utilized.

Here is an example to demonstrate the phenomenon:

Case A:

- Initial capital structure/Costs:
  —Debt interest rate = 10%
  —Tax rate = 50%
  —Debt percentage of mix = 20%
  —Equity costs = 18%
  —Equity percentage of mix = 80%
  —Weighted average cost of capital = 15.4% as follows:

  Cost of capital = $(10\% \times 50\% \times 20\%) + (18\% \times 80\%) = 15.4\%$

Case B:

- Optimal capital structure/Costs:
  —Debt interest rate = 11%
  —Tax rate = 50%
  —Debt percentage of mix = 50%
  —Equity cost = 20%
  —Equity percentage of mix = 50%
  —Weighted average cost of capital = 12.8%, as follows:

  Cost of capital = $(11\% \times 50\% \times 50\%) + (20\% \times 50\%) = 12.8\%$

Case C:

- Capital costs with too much debt:
  —Debt interest rate = 16%
  —Tax rate = 50%
  —Debt percentage of mix = 70%
  —Equity costs = 26%
  —Equity percentage of mix = 30%
  —Weighted average cost of capital = 13.4%, as follows:

  Cost of capital = $(16\% \times 50\% \times 70\%) + (26\% \times 30\%) = 13.4\%$

In moving from case ''A'' to case ''B,'' the substitution effect of increasing lower-cost debt in the capital mix from 20 percent to 50 percent more than offsets the increases in the component costs from 18 percent to 20 percent for equity, and from 10 percent to 11 percent for debt. The overall cost of capital, therefore, is reduced from 15.4 percent to 12.8 percent. Yet, in moving from case "B" to case "C," the substitution effect of further increasing lower-cost debt in the capital mix to 70 percent cannot offset the further significant increases in the component costs for this overly leveraged capital structure—from 20 percent to 26 percent for equity and from 11 percent to 16 percent for debt. The overall capital cost, therefore, moves back up to 13.4 percent.

Limitations on Debt Levels

While higher EPS or returns on equity can be achieved by using even more leverage than that in the optimal capital structure, the valuation of the firm will be reduced. Higher EPS and returns on equity will result from more debt whenever the return on assets exceeds the interest rates. The valuation, however, will always be the highest at optimal capital structure, where the minimum cost of capital will be used as the discount factor for the company's cash flows from operations so the value of the firm will be maximized.

Is it a real misunderstanding that this limit to the debt levels attributable to the additional risk is not perceived? No, this has also been well understood by both the "borrowers" and the "lenders" for some time. In fact, the "borrowers" are often overly conservative with respect to debt levels.

Back in 1982, one of the authors did a small empirical study of 150 major public companies that confirmed the extent to which higher debt percentages can reduce the cost of capital. Based upon the sample of 150 companies in 38 different industries, the 115 firms with debt/equity ratios in excess of 30 percent showed capital-cost levels of under 12 percent. The 35 companies with debt/capital ratios under 30 percent showed capital-cost levels over 14 percent.

The same study also demonstrated the difference in debt capacity among different industries. Nine of the 38 industries with the lowest capital costs were:

- Airlines
- Finance
- Hotel
- Insurance
- Medical services
- Natural gas
- Recreation/Entertainment
- Steel
- Trucking/Transportation

The businesses appeared to share a degree of capital intensity, both for tangible and intangible assets and assets likely to be marketable, apart from the success of the business.

Back in Chapter 1, we cited another fascinating, capital-intensive industry (restaurants/fast foods), and the effect that its assets may have had on price/earnings multiples. With respect to leverage, however, we can now use several experiences in this business to provide strong support for our similar conclusions about the importance of the restaurant assets to allowing high debt levels in the industry.

First, in the early 1970s, my company demonstrated the ability to finance—via debt or sale/leasebacks at a competitive rate—a major restaurant expansion program through an off-balance sheet entity and without any parental guaranty.

Second, a few years later, Pillsbury's Annual Report segregated their Burger King/Steak 'n Ale operations' capital structure from the rest of the company because of the capital intensity of the business and the lack of need for any parental guaranties for the mortgages. Of course, this made sense, since good commercial sites with relatively standard buildings are quite fungible, and other retail businesses can always utilize them.

Third, in a diversification study for another company in the soft drink industry, fast foods was targeted as a desirable candidate for acquisitions. While the returns on total capital were lower than average, debt leverage was higher than average, bringing the return on equity back to a normal level. In other words, you need more assets to run a restaurant; but the assets allow more debt financing than most businesses, so the return to the equity owners is still adequate.

The real misunderstanding about debt capacity had been, therefore, the failure to see the tremendous additional amount of leverage that can be incurred when the book values of the assets are not representative of the overall asset values. While risk had always been considered relevant, the risk that had been emphasized was the volatility of the operating performance. Yet, it now appears that the ability to maintain low costs of capital at the higher debt levels is more a function of the safety values of the assets, not of the businesses themselves.

One of the conclusions from the 1982 study was that the asset values, which are very safe over and above the book values of the assets, provide a safety net for creditors, as well as owners. If the business fails, the liquidation value of the assets should still repay many of the banks that would have been very aggressive if merely based on the operating cash flows.

To reiterate, the misunderstanding about debt capacity had been, therefore, the tremendous additional amount of leverage that can be incurred prudently when the book values of the assets are not representative of the overall asset values, apart from the value of the business. This asset effect had either been overlooked or underestimated by many "blue-chip" senior financial officers until low profits and financial problems forced some of them to pursue greater debt financing as a matter of necessity. Then, the firms with valuable hidden or under-valued assets could float the required bonds or obtain the required loans without paying more than a modest interest-rate premium and without losing what little value their stock had held. Their costs of capital, therefore, improved—not because of brilliant financial planning—but as a matter of circumstances.

Market-Value versus Book-Value Cost of Capital

It is true that the capital costs should then be calculated at market values, not book values, and that these costs will obviously be higher from the increase in the percentage of higher-cost equity. Yet, the market-value capital costs will be raised for both levels of leverage, respectively, so the conclusion to increase leverage should not be altered. Let's take a look at an example (see Table 20-1).

Table 20-1. Revalued Cost of Capital

($Millions)	Post-Tax Cost	Total Value		Percent of Total Capital		Weighted Average Cost	
		Book	Market*	Book	Market*	Book	Market*
Lower leverage							
Debt	4.5%	$ 800	$ 800	50%	20%	2.25%	0.9%
Equity	18%	800	3,200*	50%	80%	9.0%	14.4%
Total capital	N.A.	$1,600	$4,000	100%	100%	11.25%	15.3%
Higher leverage							
Debt	4.5%	$1,600	$1,600	67%	33%	3.0%	1.49%
Equity	18%	800	3,200*	33%	67%	5.94%	12.06%
Total capital	N.A.	$2,400	$4,800	100%	100%	8.96%	13.55%

*Market value of net assets and/or market value of stock is four times book value of net assets.

Now, the trend toward leveraged buyouts and/or hostile takeovers has highlighted the underestimated debt capacities. Leveraged buyouts are much more accepted as a means for managers to obtain their own businesses and for corporations to divest product lines by selling out their own managers and merely taking financial notes in payment. Takeover artists have also concentrated on the asset liquidation values in obtaining bank financing and/or utilizing junk bonds to complete their takeover deals. Then, repayment is made from the proceeds of the resold assets, and the net price of the remaining assets becomes a bargain. The key point, however, is that debt can be obtained on the front end on the basis of the asset values.

In fact, in order to fight unfriendly takeover acquisitions, it is now also common for companies to implement strategies that require much higher debt levels. The major benefit is that this uses up either the excess cash or debt capacity that could be used by ''speculative-type'' acquirers to buy the company on credit, supported by the cash or assets of the company itself. Thus, the utilization of high debt leverage has become an accepted part of both the offense and defense in the current takeover and leveraged-buyout games.

Camouflaged Leverage

Yet, most of the business-press articles, the cocktail conversationalists, and even some of the highly-paid consultants and investment bankers still seem to be missing the point. They recognize that it is a ''crime'' for some greedy speculator to buy a company with its own assets indirectly supporting the purchase, and then be left with a major piece of profit from the sale of those assets at values that were there the day before, without the slightest enhancement from any actions of the buyer. Yet, what should the company's management do to obtain the same benefit for its shareholders?

There are two fundamental valuation principles that may be involved and should be focused on separately by the company's management long before any takeover issue arises. First, assets and entire businesses may be worth more to someone else. Product-line pruning, unbundling of conglomerates, synergies with acquirers, economies of scale, and the like are all legitimate reasons for this phenomenon. These are also the ones discussed most often.

Second, and more importantly, is the effect of optimal leverage, apart from any asset liquidations. This principle, however, is discussed less often with respect to the goal of any corporation being to maximize value. This will occur only when the lowest cost of capital from the optimal capital structure is achieved. Only then will the discount rate for the company's cash flows be minimized and the present value price be maximized. Thus, when the optimal debt capacity goes unused, the cost of capital is higher than it should be, and the value of the company is less than it should be. While lowering the capital cost and raising the value (the combined value of the stock and existing debt), the cost to purchase the company is increased. Yet, the value to the shareholders is increased from the optimal use of leverage, even if no acquisition occurs, or even if no acquisition is even considered.

Asset Leverage Potential

For many major corporations, debt levels of 50 percent of total capital are reasonable. Of, course, all of this new-found knowledge would be no surprise in some industry sectors.

Real-estate investors are fully aware of the debt potential and the necessity of high leverage to yield an adequate return on equity. At Pillsbury, they have even separated their food-service operations' capital structure from the rest of the company. This is due to the significantly higher debt levels utilized and the fact that they can be obtained without the benefit of a corporate guaranty. Finally, CBS managed to finance the major portion of a music copyright joint venture with debt, based upon the stability and saleability of the tangible assets. (See Chapter 21.)

Separating Leverage from Investment Decisions

While the problem of low leverage can be solved by some corporate restructuring (for example, by means of an acquisition or stock repurchase, as discussed in Chapter 23), the evaluation of any acquisition should be done independently. There are many methods to increase leverage. You should ideally have good investments with high returns lined up. Yet, if none exist, a stock repurchase may be the answer. In any case, a bad acquisition cannot be justified merely on the grounds of adding needed leverage. The only legitimate effect that may help justifications is that the new structure will yield a lower cost of capital, and that lower cost should be used as the hurdle rate. In other words, a sow's ear cannot be made into a silk purse merely by getting a needed loan from the pig farmer.

Summary and Conclusions

The common misunderstanding about debt is the fact that high optimal debt leverage is based to a great extent upon the reduction of risk attributable to understated asset values. This debt leverage can then be used to minimize capital costs for a company and maximize valuation of the company. This is a fundamental concept in basic finance, which is now being highlighted by the realization that asset values play nearly as significant a role for corporate debt as house values do for individual home mortgages. In following through on the basics, the corporate management can help to maximize stock prices for shareholders, as well as defend against takeover raiders. The latter benefit can result even if management never directly addresses the issue of unfriendly acquisitions.

For the business-press reader and acquisition deal maker, the magnitude and pervasiveness of the new asset-based takeover phenomenon may have come as a surprise. To the soundly-based financial analyst, it should be more of a surprise that it took so long for the asset-based debt leverage to become so commonly accepted. Even today, it is still viewed by many as a separate phenomenon of the takeover artists and acquisition deal makers. Thus, this financial mistake is still with us to a great extent, and it is an excellent example of the way the basics of finance continue to be overlooked in practice.

CHAPTER 21

Cost of Digesting
Hidden Capital Increases

Problems of Low Returns on Incremental Capital

Perhaps the financial mistake of greatest concern to us is that of the failure to account for hidden capital increases in all sorts of financial decisions. It has arisen so many times in personal assignments such as acquisitions, divestitures, off-balance sheet financing, leasing, joint ventures, international investments, and financing for international subsidiaries.

Generally, there are all sorts of opportunities to increase profit returns that are really based upon the mere expansion of a company's total capital investment. The profits are derived from the funding of the incremental investment from low-cost debt funds. The returns on the investment may be quite low (well below the 25 to 30 percent pre-tax targets for most companies). Yet, if they are still above the interest rate on borrowed funds (say above 10 percent), there will still be a positive effect on profits (as discussed in Chapter 20).

Arbitrage

Perhaps the simplest and most direct example of this problem is the case of arbitrage between the markets in which you borrow and the markets in which you invest.

Not too long ago, a classic arbitrage situation arose for many American firms in Germany. Such companies could borrow at rates below the interest level being paid on very safe obligations of West German government units. Several banks were ''selling'' this opportunity. Two requirements that were likely not to be met might prevent one from proceeding with the scheme. First, there had to be *defeasance* allowed by the accountants. This would have removed both the asset and liability involved from the balance sheet, so there would be no increase in capital on which a 25 to 30 percent pre-tax return was required. Only the spread between interest income and interest expense would be reflected on the financial statements as income. Second, the rating agencies must not account for the defeased liability. This would allow no reduction in debt capacity.

Let's take a look at how defeasance was supposed to work under new FASB rules. The following was described by one of the most creative banks (one that is considered a bastion of aggressive, technical schemes to get around one regulation or another, as opposed to being an aggressive lender at low rates, a creative economic institution, or a provider of extra service):

1. *Company borrowing:*
   - $100 million debt
   - *10* percent interest expense
2. *Company investments:*
   - $100 million German government securities
   - *10.5* percent interest income
3. *Company balance sheet:*
   - No debt shown
   - No securities shown
4. *Company income statement:*
   - *1/2* percent net interest income
   - Additional $500M pre-tax income

As you can see, the income effect appears to be all gravy. There are no additional risks worthy of consideration. There are no negative effects of adding this capital at a modest return—only a 10.5 percent U.S. dollar-equivalent return. Unfortunately, our creative bankers were wrong about defeasance being allowed by the FASB accounting rules. Now, without defeasance, what are the results? Try the following:

1. *Company balance sheet:*
   - New debt of $100 million
   - New securities of $100 million
2. *Company income statement:*
   - 10 percent interest expense
   - 10.5 percent interest income
3. *Company return on investment:*
   - Incremental return on assets:
     —only 1/2 percent
   - Incremental return on capital:
     —Before interest expense
     —Still only 10.5 percent

The low returns show a poor use of the $100 million debt capacity. Again, 10.5 percent is quite poor, because when equity is added to maintain the debt/capital ratio at a target level, the weighted average cost of capital would be 25 to 30 percent pre-tax—not the 10 percent interest expense.

Exceptions to the Marginal Cost of Capital Rule

This is, of course, merely another way of stating the *marginal cost of capital concept.* Even if a 10 percent interest debt is used to finance a particular investment, the marginal cost of capital is still based upon the target combination of debt and equity, unless one of two exceptions applies . First, off-balance sheet financing may be available, such as in creative lease financing or a joint venture (both of which are discussed below). Second, a given type of asset or business may allow higher leverage, such as discussed in Chapter 20.

For the first exception of *off-balance sheet financing*, the company may elect to treat the debt service (interest and principal payments) as being the only cash outflows. This would eliminate the investment funded by the debt itself from the cash flows and from the capital investment upon which a return must be earned. Let's take a look at an example for an unconsolidated joint venture using this *leveraged approach* and compare this with our normal *capitalized approach*.

	Capitalized Approach			Leveraged Approach		
Year	Investment/ Residual	Operating Cash Flow	Post-Tax Debt Service	Investment/ Residual	Operating Cash Flow	Post-Tax Debt Service
0	(100)			0		
1		10	—		10	(5)
2		10	—		10	(5)
3		10	—		10	(5)
4		10	—		10	(5)
5		10	—		10	(5)
6		10	—		10	(5)
7		10	—		10	(5)
8		10	—		10	(5)
9		10	—		10	(5)
10	100	10	—	100	10	(105)

$$\text{NPV @ 15\%} = (\$25) \qquad \text{NPV @ 15\%} = \$25$$
$$\text{IRR} = 10\% \qquad \text{IRR} = \text{Infinite}$$

Both returns should be presented to the decision maker. The leveraged approach can never be the sole criterion, since there may be some effect of the higher leverage on the cost of capital, even if it is not consolidated. Yet, the capitalized approach would also be misleading if the off-balance sheet financing were not even identified in the footnotes to the financial statement, or if it were not treated as debt by the rating agencies and creditors.

For both exceptions, both the off-balance sheet financing and the higher-leverage assets/businesses, a new weighted average marginal cost of capital could also be used to reflect the benefits of the leveraged approach in the capitalized approach. The new cost of capital to be used is merely an adjusted capital cost or *hurdle-rate accounting for the higher-than-usual debt percentages* possible. An example of such adjustments might be the following:

1. *"Normal" cost of capital:*
- 25 percent debt/75 percent equity target ratio
- 10 percent interest rate
- 50 percent tax rate
- 20 percent required return on equity
- Cost of capital =

$$(10\% \times 50\% \times 25\%) + (20\% \times 75\%) = 1.25\% + 15\% = 16.5\%$$

2. *Off-balance sheet financing opportunity:*
- 80 percent debt at 12 percent versus 10 percent interest rate
- 20 percent equity from on-balance sheet debt and equity funds
- Cost of capital =

$$(12\% \times 50\% \times 80\%) + (20\% \times 16.5\%) = 4.8\% + 3.3\% = 9.1\%$$

3. *Higher-leverage asset investment:*
- 75 percent debt/25 percent equity target ratio
- Cost of capital =

$$(10\% \times 50\% \times 75\%) + (20\% \times 25\%) = 3.75\% + 5\% = 8.75\%$$

Under the revised capital costs of only 9% in cases 2 and 3, only a 10 percent return, which had been 6 to 7 percent lower than required, now appears quite adequate.

High-Leveraged Joint Ventures

A business-investment example, not merely a money market example, for both the leveraged approach and the capital approaches, is the syndication of a company's investment in a project. A joint venture can be set up in which the company retains only a 50 percent interest.

The majority of the cost can be funded by low-cost debt, as opposed to the small high-cost equity investments of the company and the other partners.

CBS used both of the above approaches to evaluate and justify a major investment in the lower return, but relatively safe music publishing business. The entire asset base consisted of intangible music copyrights that obviously generated cash and were resaleable. Joint-venture partners, therefore, were obtainable to supply half of the investment; in this case, the same investors also became the creditors. In fact, only the combinations of the two types of investments were sold as strips equaling 50 percent of the equity and 100 percent of the debt. From the CBS viewpoint, two evaluations were made:

1. A "leveraged-basis" internal rate of return; and
2. A "capitalized-basis" return compared against a lower-than-normal hurdle rate.

Both evaluations yielded satisfactory results.

Lease Financing

A more common type of creative financing and a common area of mistake is leasing. Since both operating and capitalized leases appear in the footnotes or body of a balance sheet, we lean towards a "capitalized approach." This means that lease commitments are merely a form of debt financing for all or a portion of capital investment and should be treated as such to evaluate both the investment and the financing elements.

A two-step process is required. First, some sort of purchase alternative must be evaluated to see if the entire investment makes any sense. Then an internal rate of return or net present value can be calculated for the entire capital investment and evaluated. This is really the same as the capitalized approach for joint ventures cited above.

Second, a buy/lease analysis should be prepared to see if the lease financing is desirable. This second step requires the calculation of the incremental cash flows of the purchase versus the lease. Then either an internal rate of return or net present value should be computed. The cost of debt, not cost of capital, is the relevant benchmark or discount rate, respectively. We prefer the former internal rate of return approach, since this return is the post-tax cost of interest being paid because it is the return given up by the lessee. The pre-tax equivalent, therefore, can be treated as the implicit interest rate in the lease, and this rate automatically accounts for all the tax benefits, residual values, and other cash-flow items, as well as the rent.

Let's take a look at Table 21-1.

Table 21-1. Buy/Lease Analysis (Inflows)/Outflows

			Year			
Purchase:	*0*	*1*	*2*	*3*	*4*	*5*
Purchase price	$1,349					
Sales tax @ 4 5/8%	62					
Total purchase price	$1,411					
Service		$ 49	$ 49	$ 49	$ 49	$ 49
Property taxes		3	3	2	2	2
Depreciation		337	289	242	193	144
Total ordinary expenses		$389	$341	$293	$244	$195
Proceeds from sales						($270)
Net book value						144
Gain on sale						($126)
Ordinary income taxes	($ 31)	($195)	($170)	($147)	($122)	($ 98)
Capital gains taxes						31
Total income taxes	($ 31)	($195)	($170)	($147)	($122)	($ 67)
Investment tax credit	$ 0					
Total costs	$1,380	$195	$170	$147	$122	$ 4
Non-cash items*	—	337	288	242	193	289
Net cash costs —purchase	$1,380	($142)	($118)	($ 95)	($ 71)	($285)

			Year			
Lease:	0	1	2	3	4	5
Rent		$ 377	$377	$377	$377	$377
Sales tax @ 4 5/8%		18	18	18	18	18
Property taxes		3	3	3	3	3
Total ordinary expenses		$ 398	$398	$398	$398	$398
Income taxes @ 50%		($ 199)	($199)	($199)	($199)	($199)
Net cash costs—lease		$ 199	$199	$199	$199	$199

Incremental Calculations:						
Net cash flows	$1,380	($341)	($317)	($294)	($270)	($484)

*Depreciation and book value upon disposition.

There is a 7 percent incremental IRR, which represents the post-tax implicit interest rate; the pre-tax equivalent is approximately 14 percent. The company's borrowing rate is 10 percent, as seen in the post-tax cost of debt used of 5 percent. The lessee, therefore, will pay a 4 percent interest premium for the lease financing over the normal debt financing alternatives.

We prefer this *implicit-interest approach*, where the premium can be compared with any special benefits of leasing, since a higher rate than debt interest may be more than justified by leasing benefits. Obsolescence may be avoided. Service may also be a factor. Sometimes, one may have to pay a small premium for leasing an ice machine, since the only maintenance contract available locally is with the lessor. Of course, there is always the accounting advantages of off-balance sheet treatment whenever the lease can be constructed to avoid capitalization.

Under FASB rules, a shorter term than the useful life or a significant market-value purchase option at the end of the lease may avoid having a lease capitalized. If a lease remains off the balance sheet, and if there are no rating agency or creditor adjustments made in evaluating the company's debt/equity ratio, additional debt capacity will have been created, and then lower-cost debt will have been substituted for high-cost equity in the capital structure.

That brings us back to the main theme of the cost of hidden capital. The calculations in the second step cited above use the cost of debt as the relevant benchmark or discount rate, *not* the cost of capital. If the debt cost were used in the first step, it would be analogous to forgetting the weighted average capital being spent with "borrowed funds" when a lease commitment is made. Using a cost of capital in the second step—the buy/lease comparison—would also be no different from merely using the lease cash flow in the first step in a "leveraged-basis" analysis versus a "capitalized-basis" analysis. This would again not consider the purchase-alternative value as that would yield a lower capitalized value of the debt commitment implicit in the lease by using the higher cost of capital versus the lower cost of debt.

In any case, most projections would look good on a "leveraged-approach" basis in the first step. Also, most leases would show implicit interest rates well below the cost of capital in the buy/lease comparison of the second step. Yet, the capitalized approach and the debt-rate benchmarks, respectively, are the only ones relevant for the two steps if the lessee company is on the hook for all the risk and all the liability of the lease commitment from the outset. After all, lease financing, as well as other debt financing, is cheaper than equity financing; but there is a limit to the amount of low-cost debt that can be utilized in the optimal capital structure or debt/capital ratio. Thus, the cost of all the commitment funds should be at a weighted average of high-cost equity and low-cost debt. Only if the risk is transferred to the lessor would the non-capitalization make sense and justify the use of the leveraged approach in step one and the cost of capital as the capitalization-rate benchmark in step two.

We can point to many examples in our personal experience where leasing decisions were highly dependent on the accounting treatment received for capitalizing or not capitalizing the lease. We do feel that there is a qualitative benefit of a lease that is not capitalized, and this may prove to be significant enough to justify paying a premium over debt cost to obtain such a lease. Yet, in the long run, most creditors will evaluate most leases, whether or not capitalized, as a fixed-charge commitment that will limit further debt capacity. This means that our normal two-step approach to evaluate leases, which was outlined above, should be used to determine what premium over debt cost is being paid and how much it is really worth to a given corporation at a given time.

Hidden Acquisition Financing

Now that you have become leasing experts, let's move on to what is probably the most glowing example of this "free-lunch" syndrome. Many more than one acquisition proposal ignores either or both of existing debt in the acquired company and seller financing of the acquisition itself. It is obvious that if we go to the bank for loan funds to acquire another company, this is merely part of the overall financing done by the corporation for its expansion programs, including acquisitions. The marginal cost of capital, used as the benchmark for internal rate of return calculations, does not mean that the bank interest rate is the relevant capital cost. A weighted average cost over time or at some target debt/capital ratio is envisioned in the marginal concept. Yet, if the financing is more directly related to the acquisition, somehow it becomes regarded as no up-front commitment of capital.

Debt service for existing debt is often treated as merely one of several elements of cash outflows and disregarded in the initial investment requirements for the acquisition itself. Similarly, direct financing from the seller is somehow viewed as being different from other financing done by the acquiring company, merely because it is done as part of the acquisition. Yet, these examples should not be excluded from total capital investment requirements any more than a mortgage on a new plant can be excluded. Rather, they should be included as debt components in the overall capital structure, and the return calculations should incorporate them under the *capitalized-basis approach*.

There are also several less obvious types of acquisition financing to be considered. Management contracts with employees not required, or no longer required, to run the business, and management contracts including compensation and perquisites above the market rates for the positions involved are prime examples of purchase-financing commitments. They are made to induce the sale of the company whether the recipients are owners or not. The proper measure for the debt being incurred and capital being spent is the present value, at the cost of debt, of the post-tax payments over and above the needs of the business.

Contingency payments or *earn-out contracts* are another example of hidden leverage in acquisition deals. If the payments are relatively fixed, if they vary with something other than earnings, or if a significant portion is nearly "guaranteed" under normal expectations, then such payments are really a part of the purchase price and initial debt being assumed. Again, the expected present value of the post-tax cash flows is the relevant amount to be used.

Let's take a look at two examples of the calculations involved (see Tables 21-2 and 21-3).

Table 21-2. Example for Loan with Interest

		Project Years				
	0	*1*	*2*	*3*	*4*	*5*
Downpayment	$5,000	—	—	—	—	—
Principal	—	—	—	—	—	$10,000
Interest @ 10%	—	$1,000	$1,000	$1,000	$1,000	$ 1,000
Tax credit for interest	—	(500)	(500)	(500)	(500)	(500)
Net cash outflows	$5,000	$ 500	$ 500	$ 500	$ 500	$10,500

Present value to be calculated in purchase price = $14,600.*

Table 21-3. Example for Contingency Payment

		Project Years				
	0	*1*	*2*	*3*	*4*	*5*
Initial Payment	$5,000	—	—	—	—	—
Contingent Payment	—	—	—	—	—	$10,000
Interest	—	—	—	—	—	—
Tax credit	—	—	—	—	—	(5,000)
Imputed interest	—	—	—	—	—	—
Net cash outflow	$5,000	—	—	—	—	$ 5,000

Present value to be calculated in purchase price = $8,726.*

*At 6% post-tax cost of debt.

Perhaps the best argument for the capitalized approach being proposed is that the seller or management could always have required more of an initial purchase price in lieu of the contractual payments. Similarly, one or both of them choose an earn-out structure for tax benefits obtained by one or both sides. There are also deal-structure benefits to an earn-out contract, if the seller is convinced that growth projections are in the bag and the buyer remembers "caveat emptor" from his school days. Nevertheless, a debt commitment is being made on the front end for future payments.

There are arguments, however, that do support a leveraged approach. The best of them may cite the effects on the consolidated post-acquisition balance sheet. Will any portion of the management contracts or earn-outs be reflected? To the extent a portion of the payments do not adversely affect the debt/capital and/or fixed-charge-coverage ratios, such as the rating agency and creditor ratings, then there may be no practical effect of the economic reality of the liability. In such cases, I would again take a look at both capitalized and leveraged calculations. After all, the portion of the price not reflected on the balance sheet is analogous to off-balance sheet leasing, and we have already decided that this benefit should be identified and might be worth a lease-interest premium.

Treasury Operations

Now let's turn to a group of Treasurer-type, hidden-capital examples. First, discounts taken by the consumer or given by the supplier for early payment of trade payables must be converted to an annual effective interest rate on income earned or expense incurred. For example, if the trade terms are 2/10 net 30, payment is due in 30 days. But the payment is usually delayed until 60 days by an aggressive controller, and a two percent discount is given for payment within 10 days. The following formula does the job:

$$\text{Opportunity cost} = 2/98 \times [360/(60-10)] = 15\%$$

This pre-tax effective interest rate, however, cannot be compared with the bank interest rate on money borrowed to fund the payment or that which could have been earned if money had been retained and deposited. The net outflows or proceeds are reductions from or additions to the company's total capital level; as such, they must be compared with the company's required return on capital, or its pre-tax cost of capital. In this case, the discount should not be taken because it is below the normal 25 to 30 percent required pre-tax return on capital as a result of the tremendous 50-day lag, or use of interest-free money that would be foregone.

Similarly, to the extent interest-free or low-interest compensating balances are still used in conjunction with loans and other bank services—this is still especially common under some foreign banking practices—the cost of the balances is not merely the interest lost. The opportunity cost, such as a 25 to 30 percent pre-tax cost of capital, represents the real cost, for the same reasons discussed with respect to all the other examples in this chapter. The addition to the capital requirements must be assumed to come from both debt and equity sources in an optimal mix (namely, in the capital-structure target mix); and the cost, therefore, is obviously the weighted average cost of capital.

Let's take a look at the difference this approach can make in calculating a cost percentage:

1. Calculate the effective annual interest-cost yield or percent based, excluding the effect of any compensating balance (for example, the ten percent rate charged by the bank).

2. Calculate the weighted average of that effective rate on the face amount of the debt and the pre-tax cost of capital, less any interest received on the compensating balance increase in capital requirements. For example, for 15 percent interest-free compensating balances, the calculation would be:

$$(10\% \times 100\%/115\%) + [(30\% - 0\%) \times (15\%/115\%)]$$
$$= 8.7\% + 3.9\% = 12.6\%$$

Please note that this 12.6 is a full 2.6 percent, or 260 basis points, higher than the face rate. All bankers and Treasury investors would consider such an increment to be huge. This result is also at lease 80 basis points above the effective yield on a discounted-basis approach (similar to those used in Chapter 15). The latter would have been 11.8 percent if net proceeds of only 85 percent were available to the company during the loan:

$$10\%/85\% = 11.8\%$$

Did we then make a mistake in Chapter 15 in calculating the higher yields or interest costs attributable to bond discounts and issuance expenses? Did we fail to account for the impact of higher capital required at the higher cost of capital? We do not believe so because of the different effects on the balance sheet.

Bond discounts and front-end commissions and closing costs on loans/issues are all reflected on the balance sheet as if they were prepaid interest expenses. The debt principal amount is shown as equal to the net proceeds. Neither the debt amount nor the debt/capital ratio is distorted. The front-end costs are merely amortized and charged to interest expense over the life of the debt. There is no reduction of debt capacity, therefore, beyond the principal amount of the loan shown on a net-proceeds basis. Unlike compensating balances, discounts and front-end commissions add to the interest rate, but not to the amount of debt itself.

Blocked-Funds Repatriation

The next type of hidden capital is in the area of *blocked-funds repatriation*. When a company's foreign cash is blocked by legal prohibitions, or tax penalties occur for repatriation, then all sorts of parallel loan variations are proposed by our ever-helpful bankers. As shown in Chapter 14, unless the two halves of the transaction can be linked by a right of set-off (which is usually illegal or defeats the tax purpose), then accounting defeasance cannot be obtained for the new loan receivable and loan payable on the corporate books. Without defeasance, what do we get? More hidden capital.

For a consolidated subsidiary, a parallel loan merely transfers foreign cash into a loan receivable, and a loan payable is added domestically. The latter will add to capital if deposited as excess cash and will thus be more than a neutral capital-level factor, unless existing loans are retired with excess cash. For a deconsolidated subsidiary, the domestic loan is the only transaction reflected on the balance sheet. In both cases, however, the failure to reduce capital by bringing cash home defeats the purpose. We are then left with either an increase of cash earning money market rates, when three times as high a cost of capital is required, or a mere replacement of one loan by another. This is the same as the arbitrage situations we discussed earlier.

Yet, despite all of the above analyses, many experts in the field do try to market parallel loans as a means of repatriating excess cash that is blocked in a given foreign country. Many such proposals, for example, were made vis-à-vis CBS' excess Greek drachma, as cited in Chapter 14.

Subsidized Loans

Let's take a look at different types of situations where free lunches are indeed being served regularly. For starters, many governments do give subsidized loans for investments in "socially desirable" projects. Now, even if a company plans to fund all or part of its investment with retained earnings, the favorable rate borrowing can be used to replace other debt to lower the company's overall cost of debt, and thus the cost of total capital funds. Only if the proceeds will wind up generating or retaining more excess cash will there be a hidden capital-cost problem. Of course, for a properly leveraged company, there is always some debt on the books to be replaced at the bargain rates.

Similarly, many acquisition sellers are willing to give favorable financing. Also, some companies have low-cost debt on their balance sheets that can be assumed by the buyer. While we have already stated that both sources of funds should be considered part of the capital investment, the low rates must not be overlooked.

For all of this subsidized financing from the government or acquisitions, the lower debt cost should technically be included as the debt component in the cost-of-debt calculations to be used as the discount rate for the subsidized project. An alternative method could also be used, however, to achieve the same result. We could discount the subsidized debt interest and principal payments at the normal cost of debt in order to yield a reduced present value. This will reduce the initial capital cost, thus benefiting the net present value calculation for the interest-rate savings calculation. For example, in the extreme example of a zero-interest loan, $15,000 can be borrowed with a present value equivalent of only $11,000, as follows:

		Project Years				
	0	1	2	3	4	5
Principal	$5,000	—	—	—	—	$10,000
Interest	—	—	—	—	—	—
Tax credit for IRS imputed interest	—	($350)	($350)	($350)	($350)	(350)
Net cash outflows	$5,000	($350)	($350)	($350)	($350)	$ 9,650

Present value to be calculated in purchase price = $11,000.*

*At 6% post-tax cost of debt.

Intercompany Loans

There is also another type of "free lunch" available. *Intercompany loans* do not involve hidden capital being retained on the balance sheet because the loan payable and receivable are eliminated upon consolidation. Thus, some excess cash that is blocked, but not by foreign exchange controls, can be repatriated. Bank account overdrafts by one operation within an overall bank pool for the whole company have a similar effect. These examples, therefore, are exceptions to the general caveats stated for parallel loans—the same as defeasance.

Summary and Conclusions

There are indeed very few "free lunches" around in finance. Off-balance sheet items should be utilized to access interest-free sources of funds. Joint ventures may be one emerging area of lower capital requirements and higher-than-normal returns. Lease financing is another device for minimizing capital costs. The same approach can be followed in acquisitions.

Yet, capitalizing all of the debt as part of the total investment should be done for at least one of the calculations of a project's return. Funds from subsidiary operations and government priority sectors, however, should be used as a genuine "free lunch" where possible. In such cases, there can be definite reductions from normal capital costs to justify projects with lower returns.

CHAPTER 22

Foreign Subsidiary Capital Structures

General Worldwide Capital-Structure Goals

In Chapter 20, we discussed the goal of a capital-structure decision as being increased debt in the debt/equity mix to a point where the substitution effect of replacing high-cost equity (18 to 20 percent) with low-cost debt (5 to 6 percent post-tax) is offset by the increase in both the interest rates charged by lenders and the returns required by shareholders. These increases are attributable to the increased risk to both lenders and shareholders resulting from the higher debt leverage utilized and its effect on the volatility of earnings.

Is this not equally applicable to foreign corporations? Of course it is. And is this not equally applicable to the foreign subsidiaries of a multinational parent corporation? Of course it is *not*.

Foreign Capital-Structure Goals

Keep in mind that the capital-structure decision of the optimal debt/equity mix must be made at the overall corporate level where all of the firm's resources and financing are consolidated. The choice of deriving a portion of the debt from one place and a portion of the equity from another place is a much different type of decision.

The goals for this financing allocation decision are basically of four types:

1. *Flexibility*—for ease of future financing decisions and cash utilization.
2. *Management psychology*—for motivation of the local subsidiary management to control the balance sheet investments while competing aggressively against competitors in the local marketplace.
3. *Bank relations*—for satisfying local banking practices to achieve adequate lines of credit and banking services, especially where there is no worldwide relationship between the bank and/or its parent and the multinational parent of the subsidiary.
4. *Government politics*—for satisfying the minimum equity investment requirements for both legal and political purposes.

For all of the above goals, one common theme might be *commitment*. The multinational parent corporation must demonstrate commitment to standing behind local subsidiary debts and funding the local subsidiary operating requirements when they exist. The former is really quite easy to demonstrate with comfort letters, and even guaranty letters, given to local banks by the parent company.

A parent company's track record in the given country, or other countries, in standing behind its subsidiaries and in ensuring their adequate funding, will be of help. Also, if a subsidiary's business is obviously valuable, then it may be easier to demonstrate commitment. For losing operations with little equity funding, however, commitment can become a quite legitimate issue for the local governments and unions, even if the banks and creditors can be satisfied, or legally safeguarded, as to their creditor risks.

Favorable Foreign Capital Markets

Did you notice that we never said low-cost debt was an issue? Well, most multinational corporations should separate the analysis of debt markets, or where to borrow (in terms of interest rates, availability of funds, and structural options/covenants), from the decision on who should borrow, either the parent corporation or a subsidiary. Even if a local, foreign borrowing is deemed advantageous (see Chapter 21), and even if a subsidiary entity is used to consumate the deal for some legal or tax reasons, financing local subsidiary needs is still a separate decision. It is this latter financing decision that is addressed in this chapter. Since most local foreign subsidiaries do not have a multinational reputation by themselves, unlike the parent company, borrowing outside the local foreign markets should not be considered, with the exception of inter-company loans.

Alternative Approaches

What are the specific alternative policies used by different multi-national firms to finance their foreign subsidiaries? Well, there are at least four worth outlining:

1. *Autonomous approach*—Set debt and equity levels for each subsidiary that will yield acceptable debt/capital, earnings-coveraged, and fixed-charged-coveraged ratios compared with other companies in the given country and, especially, with local competitors in the given country in the same industry.

2. *Minimum-equity level*—Finance all foreign capital funding requirements with local foreign debt first. Then continue with intercompany debt, except for the minimum amount of equity that is designated by law, tax considerations, and/or local banks.

3. *Operating/strategic decision classification*—Finance all long-term asset requirements with equity and all net working capital requirements with debt.

4. *ROE target*—Set ROE target for each local foreign operation equal to corporate target after covering interest expense, adjusted for local risk levels.

Perhaps the following examples will help clarify the differences:

Assumptions

- Local/competitor debt/capital ratios = 40%
- Legal minimum-equity level = 20% total assets
- Total assets = $100, $50 fixed and $50 current
- Trade payables = $25
- Profit before interest after taxes = $10
- Post-tax interest = 5%
- ROE target = 20%

Capital Structure

	Debt	Equity	Debt/Capital* Ratio(%)
Autonomous	$30	$45	40
debt = 40% × $75*			
Minimum equity	55	20	73
equity = 20% × $100			
Operating decision	25	50	33
equity = $50			
ROE target	33	42	44
ROE = ($10 − $1.65)/$42			

*Capital = Total assets less interest-free liabilities.

For an efficient corporate financial policy, the *minimum-equity approach* would provide repatriation flexibility. When excess cash is created over and above local operating needs, funds can immediately be used to reduce the consolidated corporate capital by repaying the debt. Even if no dividend remittance capacity exists, debt can usually be repaid, especially to local banks. The reduced debt means reduced overall capital; the savings will be at the full cost of capital, not merely the lower cost of debt. This nearly always exceeds local interest income on investments of the excess cash.

The other three approaches could also represent three worthwhile philosophies:

1. *Autonomous approach*—Gives local management the same return-on-investment and interest-cost perspectives for pricing and other decisions as their competitors and local peer groups.

2. *Operating/strategic classification*—Gives local management the emphasis on the part of the balance sheet they can and should control and removes their concern for the equity-funded remaining portion.

3. *ROE target*—Not really a financial target, but a rationalization to show your local managers that they can still attain adequate profitability, or returns on equity, despite a given debt level. If an adequate ROE cannot be obtained because debt or equity is too high (usually the latter), return on capital might also be too much of a disincentive for local managers.

Special Strategies for Specific Countries

There are two types of strategies that may alter your decision among the alternative approaches to foreign capital structures. Minimum equity may become even more desirable whenever a country is considered to have a blocked-currency situation. Minimum debt may become quite desirable whenever it can be shown that real interest rates are high, apart from any risk shifting towards the creditors.

In Greece and Eastern Europe, for example, blocked funds have been the normal situation for many years. American multinational corporations, therefore, that require a full-blown local operation to do business, should seriously consider limiting any equity infusion to the minimum level that local government regulations and banking practices permit. Cash generated locally can then at least be used to repay debt and to provide future financing.

In hyper-inflationary Latin American countries (such as Brazil, Argentina, and Mexico), minimum debt levels should be considered. There have been times when the high local interest rates are also high on a real basis after adjusting for high local inflation rates. A similar adjustment would be to calculate dollar-equivalent interest rates after high devaluation of the local-currency principal and interest obligations against the dollar. The uncertainty surrounding the general economic situations, outlook for future interest rates, inflation, and currency devaluation supposedly has had the effect of increasing real interest rates, at least during some recent periods of time. Some ex post empirical analysis has been presented to prove this. Yet we must be very cautious in developing any strategy aimed at minimizing debt and replacing it with equity in a hyper-inflationary country for at least three reasons!

1. Ex ante expectations and forecasts are volatile and may not accurately predict the ex post real interest calculations.

2. Interest-free equity may lessen management's concern with minimizing investment in assets that can rapidly devaluate in dollar terms, unless they are held equally responsible for foreign exchange translation losses on assets as they are for interest expense.

3. Even if high real interest rates prevail at some period of time, market forces should bring them down, or at least diminish the excess real levels in the long term.

Foreign Subsidiary Dividend Policy

Assuming you have chosen your favorite approach, let's see what the implications are for some of the parent company's major international financial policies. For subsidiary dividends to the parent company, if you are committed to any of four approaches, then the dividend levels set for your subsidiaries will be a fall-out of that capital-structure target (namely, the earnings and investment-requirement levels).

This is analogous to the residual theory of dividends outlined in Chapter 24 as the basis for dividends for any corporation with its shareholders. Yet, remember that there is still a major difference between the overall corporate strategy and that of foreign subsidiaries. The capital structure for subsidiaries is not aimed at the lowest cost of capital, which is the proper goal for any corporation; but instead, it is aimed at fulfilling one of the four approaches outlined earlier.

One six-step system designed for foreign subsidiaries may help clarify matters, as follows:

1. *Calculate effective equity level* by adding capital stock, retained earnings, and interest-free intercompany liabilities.

2. *Define normal equity level* as a minimum level of equity, or one of the other targets, such as the non-current asset level.

3. *Calculate excess deficiency* of equity by subtracting the normal equity in (#2) from the company's effective equity in (#1).

4. *Designate dividends to be declared:*
   - *Total* equals excess equity in (#3).
   - *Deficiency*, or negative excess in (#3), may require either an equity infusion versus a dividend or merely a deferral of a dividend until an excess position is attained.
   - *External dividend* is the maximum portion of the total that can legally be declared by the legal entity to the parent company or any other affiliates which is the immediate parent of the subsidiary.
   - *Internal dividend* is the remaining portion of the total to be designated as corporate division funds on special internal financial statements to be prepared locally and/or by the parent.

5. *Financing of both internal/external dividends* should be done from one of the following in order of priority:
   - Excess cash
   - Intercompany loan from corporate division
   - Intercompany loans from affiliates
   - Overdraft/bank debt to extent normal equity level in (#2) is maintained (even after the cash proceeds from the additional debt are used to pay dividends)

6. *Internal dividends usage* by the corporate division would in turn be for the following:
   - Paying dividends up to the legal capacity in any country without excess cash
   - Intercompany loans to other affiliates requiring cash, other working capital, or PP&E
   - Intercompany loans to the parent company for temporary peak-period working capital requirements

197

Foreign Working Capital Management

Another group of decisions impacted by capital-structure philosophy is the local working capital management. To the extent that equity cash builds up more easily, this raises the minimum level required to run the business, contrary to the goal cited in Chapter 2. The local management will not see any cost for the working capital funded by equity. For receivables and inventories they will also see either no cost, or at most, the lost interest on bank deposits, which could be much less than the borrowing cost for funds. Minimum-equity levels or a non-current asset equity level would prevent this type of problem. Of course, local management really should treat the cost of working capital as the cost of capital, which is much higher than interest costs and applies to all funds, whether borrowed or not.

Foreign Manager Perspectives

While this analysis of the capital structure and its implications is fairly straightforward, local financial management, especially in foreign countries, may not identify with it. For example, we know that the real cost of funds retained by subsidiaries is the cost of capital and that a mere interest charge on local financial statements is really very generous.

Yet, we have heard intelligent local managers say how they cannot afford to borrow money for their working capital needs because they cannot cover the interest expense. Well, you know they then should usually not invest the money because covering about three times the interest expense is required for an adequate return. That is why a rationalization or political compromise may be necessary to sell any capital control program to local management.

One such sales approach we discussed was the debt level that still allowed an overall ROE target to be met. Of course, you may be forced to come up with other ones to sell any of the other three approaches we discussed. Remember, many local managers feel the best capital structure is always to use 100 percent interest-free funding.

Summary and Conclusions

The true capital-structure decision must be made at the overall corporate level. Yet, the financing and dividend policies for each subsidiary should be based on flexibility, management psychology, bank relations, and government politics. We would emphasize the flexibility goal, in terms of avoiding any buildup of excess cash and, thus, total capital. Local interest rates are relevant only when they are high in dollar-equivalent terms, which is rarely true, except in hyper-inflation countries.

Hidden Benefits of Additional Leverage in Corporate Restructures

Leverage in Corporate Restructuring

We have all heard so much lately about the increased emphasis on the major restructuring of corporate finances and business portfolios. It is being treated as some new and independent phenomenon by the business press and some members of the consulting and investment banking community. The increased emphasis does exist and cannot be denied. Yet, the basic elements of the restructuring are nothing more than the sound fundamentals of financial and strategic planning that have been practiced, by at least some companies, and espoused by many professional planners and analysts for a number of years.

In terms of financial planning, the major element underlying all the hoopla is merely financial leverage. The benefits of high leverage were broadly discussed in Chapter 20. Now in this chapter it emerges as the cornerstone of the latest, most effective corporate restructuring strategies.

Types of Corporate Restructures

Perhaps we should start off with a definition. *Corporate restructuring* can be defined generally as the redeployment of assets on the left-hand side of the balance sheet and the utilization of new sources to fund these assets on the right-hand side. Pragmatically, there are several major strategies encompassed:

- Acquisitions
- Divestitures
- Debt financing
- Creative off-balance sheet financing
- Stock repurchases

Financial Elements of Corporate Restructures

Apart from the strategic planning factors, there are three major elements of the financial strategy:

1. Optimal degree of leverage for the lowest cost of capital
2. Off-balance sheet leverage leaving the cost of capital relatively unaffected
3. Disposition of underutilized assets, in terms of low returns on market-value opportunity costs

The last element was discussed at length in Chapters 10 and 20 as a major factor in the recent acquisition/takeover phenomenon. The second element of creative financing was discussed indirectly in Chapter 21, as a possible exception to the cost of hidden capital increase through additional leverage when debt remains off the balance sheet. The first element, however, is the most significant for the recent restructuring trends alluded to in Chapter 20, and it represents the primary subject of this chapter.

Segregating Leverage Effects

Let me restate the basic rule. A capital structure should be set with debt levels high enough to reduce the weighted average cost of total capital funds to the lowest level. When any corporate restructuring, therefore, increases leverage towards such an optimal level without going beyond that optimal level, the cost of capital is reduced. As stated before, this lowers the discount rate for all the future cash flows of the corporation, thereby increasing the present value. In evaluating the purposes and effects of any restructuring, therefore, we must be sure to see if this additional financial leverage is the major, if not the only, factor to be monitored.

Two prime examples of this phenomenon are *acquisitions* and *stock repurchase*. The latter is very much in vogue and is often misunderstood, both in its use as an anti-takeover device and as a more general device to increase shareholder satisfaction with the present management. The press often concentrates on only two special aspects as if they were the critical ones:

1. Capital gains for selling shareholders in a tender offer (if a higher-than-market price is offered)
2. Purchase of shares from neutral shareholders leaving greater percentage in friendly hands

Yet, neither of these factors may be critical for the following reasons:

- *Special dividend effects,* because capital gains from higher-than-market prices merely represent an alternative to higher dividends for returning more value to the shareholders.
- *Unfriendly-hands ownership percentages can actually increase* because a widely-held ownership is somewhat of an anti-takeover safeguard, and if neutral shareholders tender, then unfriendly shareholders may need to purchase even less stock to gain control.

Neither of these factors emphasize the basic financial explanation of successful results for a stock repurchase strategy to obtain shareholder satisfaction and to deter some unfriendly takeovers. So let's get to the heart of the issue that is most likely to clarify the major portion of results.

The stock repurchases at a high price—or even at a market price—are funded by using excess cash or incurring extra debt leverage. To the extent this brings us closer to an optimal capital structure, capital costs decrease, the discount rate decreases, and the present value of the company or the stock price increases. A more direct way to look at the phenomenon is that the excess cash or excess debt capacity is finally being utilized. When this cannot be done with some major expansion program, because such opportunities cannot be found at appropriate return and risk levels, then stock repurchases are the next answer.

Now, once the extra value is realized from the optimal leverage, and the excess cash or debt capacity is removed, then many unfriendly takeover artists will lose their edge and/or desire. If junk bonds, supported by excess debt capacity, are a primary means of financing, then their support will be reduced or removed. If a cash takeover at a premium price, supported by the extra liquidation value of the assets or business, is planned, then that value will be reduced or removed.

Stock Repurchases

The increase in value perhaps can best be shown by the following sequence:

1. EPS will increase:
   - If the repurchase-price price/earnings ratio is less than the reciprocal of the post-tax interest rate on funds borrowed to make the repurchase, then the effect of the reduction in shares more than offsets the decrease in earnings caused by the increase in interest expense
2. Price per share will increase:
   - If the price/earnings ratio does not decline more than the EPS increases
   - The same as the net reduction in the cost of capital, when the increase in the debt and equity is not more than the substitution effect of lower-cost for higher-cost debt
3. Total value to shareholder increases if:
   - price per share increases for remaining shares
   - repurchased shares sold at prior market value

- The same as the reduction in value to a potential takeover buyer, who must buy remaining shares at a higher price and still assume the same amount of debt as the value of the repurchased shares

There may be some distortion of this valuation concept, however, when analyzing the post-repurchase stock-price trends. Yet, if we keep in mind the reasons to expect a stock-price decline, despite the increase in value attributable to leverage, and if we identify the other factors that change stock prices both up and down, then we can compare the actual trend with an expected or adjusted price target.

Again, let's look at an example. The analysis in Table 23-1 of the 1985 CBS stock repurchase shows that exchange offer may have been quite successful in terms of fundamental valuation because of increased leverage. The approximate data and the expected price-per-share decline were taken from the financial press' reporting of Wall Street's assessment before the repurchase. Since the post-repurchase price rose rapidly, despite the removal of some takeover speculation that reduces stock prices, the shareholder values may have been aided merely by higher leverage.

The other prime example of the benefits of increased leverage in corporate restructuring, from the more optimal capital structure that can be achieved, is acquisitions. By purchasing another company, any one or more of the following can add to leverage:

- Use of excess cash for purchase price
- Use of new debt for purchase price
- Assumption of acquired company's debt on new, consolidated balance sheet (adds to leverage only if debt/equity exceeds that of acquiring company)

The post-acquisition value of the buyer corporation will then be a function of two separate and independent factors:

1. Market value of new businesses to buyer over/under the purchase price:
   - Accounting for net purchase price for remaining assets after any liquidations of other assets

Table 23-1. Analysis of Exchange Offer

Stock Price and Economic Effects of Increased Leverage

Summary Analysis

Current price of stock
Less: Expected price of stock
Equals: Effect of leverage
—Also real economic value of entire repurchase

Expected Price Change without Leverage Effects

—Pre-repurchase price of $115
Less: "Special dividend" effect*
—Repurchase $150 versus market price of $115 is equivalent to one-time dividend of the difference for 21 percent of the shares, or approximately $7 for each original share or $9 for each remaining share.** This equals more than two years worth of extra dividends, which are also taxed at only capital gains tax rates to the shareholders. As with any dividend, the value removed from the company reduces the remaining value, apart from any investor-relation implication and leverage.
Add or Less: Effect of operating/results outlook change, reduced earnings, ratings, and increase writeoffs
Less: Takeover speculation removed
Add or Less: Stock market trends
Equals: Expected price of stock

*Special dividend effect–Four perspectives:

1. Total company—Same as full $150 times 21 percent of shares or $31.50.

2. Tendering shareholder—In terms of money received (93 percent of shareholders), same as full $150 times pro rata effective 25 percent of shares or $37.50. In terms of money received, without change of ownership, it is $31.50 per original shares.

3. Non-tendering shareholder—Same as loss in value in #4 below.

**4. Per-share basis—New value equals:

$$[\text{original } \$115 \text{ market price} - (\$115 \times 21\%)]/79\% = \$106$$

which is $9 less than original per-share price of $115.

- Adding to the purchase price, any debt assumed or obtained by the buyer, including that obtained from the seller

2. Effect of higher leverage on the cost of capital (discount rate) and

present value of all post-acquisition cash flows from the assets and business of buyer

Be aware of a criteria caveat, however. These two factors must be kept separate when the decisions are made. While it is true that an acquisition can yield increases in value of the buyer corporation merely from the additional leverage—even when no synergies exist and even when the purchase price exceeds the market value of the acquired company—the acquisition must be kept as a separate decision. Yet, why lose value on the first factor—the acquisition itself—merely to obtain the second factor, namely, additional leverage? If good acquisitions or internal expansion programs cannot be found, then a stock repurchase program is always available to yield the desired increase in debt leverage. Such an approach is always preferable to the alternatives of maintaining excess cash/debt capacity or making an overpriced/poor-fit acquisition.

Summary and Conclusions

While the acquisition and leverage decisions must be kept separate, the latter may explain the favorable market reactions to some of the recently announced acquisitions. These are the ones that appear to be priced at a premium without any perceived synergies. Remember, the market will automatically evaluate any increase in leverage, as well as the acquisition itself, and the impact of each valuation will show up in one combined post-acquisition stock price.

CHAPTER 24

Dividend Levels and Policy

Ultimate Importance of Dividends

What makes the world go around? There is no doubt that in corporate valuation or the stock market, dividends or dividend potential is the driving force.

As stated way back in Chapter 1, dividends are the basis for the valuation of corporations as reflected in the stock price. (Please note we are talking only about cash dividends, for the reasons discussed in Chapter 6.) This holds both for the long-term, low-turnover shareholder and the active investor seeking capital gains. As shown in Chapter 1, near-term capital gains are the function of the outlook for long-term dividend potential, so the *dividend-growth-in-perpetuity model* should reflect the fundamental value of a given stock.

De-emphasis on a High-Dividend Policy

Well then, if dividends make the world go around, then it must be good to pay high dividends, right? Also, a dividend policy must be one of the most important ones for a company, right? By now you know, of course, that neither statement is fully true.

Once all your investment decisions are made, you have already determined the amount of capital to be brought into and retained within the company. Then, when the optimal degree of leverage is established, as discussed in Chapter 20, the amount of dividends to be paid to the amount of new equity to be sold, namely the *dividend yield,* will automatically fall out. This, of course, is the classic *residual theory of dividends.*

Dividend policies must obviously be set for some financial planning horizon—whether one year or the long term—rather on a project-by-project basis or even on a quarter-by-quarter basis. If so, what types of companies should expect to pay high dividends? Why, of course, companies with lots of good investment opportunities. And what are such companies called? Why, *growth companies,* of course.

Yet, some businesses are not capital intensive in terms of fixed assets or net working capital requirements and can be grown without much investment. So capital-intensive growth companies should indeed expect to pay little or no dividends during their rapid-growth period. Similarly, shareholders should expect, and even desire, to receive little or no dividends during this period. Now, who then should pay high dividends? Why, of course, cash-rich, low-growth companies. While these firms may be financially sound and quite profitable, they still do not possess the investment opportunities that justify retaining a large portion of their earnings. Their shareholders should understand this, and they probably even selected the company's stock with high dividend payments in mind.

In other words, we should be setting a dividend policy that does fall out of our other financial decisions and is based upon the residual theory. Yet, this policy should be applied over a financial planning horizon, so that it will be consistent with stable dividends or stable dividend increases over that time period.

Is this policy, or indeed any dividend policy, a critical one by itself—apart from any impacts it has on the investment decisions or the optimal capital structure? It is certainly important, but not really critical. While differentiating the cash retention needs of capital-intensive growth companies from those of non-capital-intensive and/or non-growth companies is indeed critical, this is done automatically in the long run through the residual theory with the application of the appropriate investment and capital-structure decisions. Using this input, therefore, to develop a specific dividend policy, is a good idea, but not absolutely necessary.

Emphasis on Change in Dividend Policy

Yet, what if the residual theory does not account for all the effects of dividends on the value of the company, and thus its share price? Can a dividend policy affect such valuation apart from our investment/capital-structure decision process? This concept is called the *relevancy theory* and states that dividend levels and dividend policy are relevant for maximization of the company's value all by themselves.

At least, some empirical evidence supports this latter school of thought. The consensus, therefore, appears to support some relevancy of dividend policy, even though the main factor affecting the value of a company and the price of its stock must be the basic fundamentals of finance incorporated into the residual theory.

This is a supportable consensus, but the mistake is perhaps in concentrating too much on setting any dividend policy. The key element of dividend decisions is knowing when to change the policy in place. In other words, we first utilize the residual theory when originally setting a dividend policy and when deciding on the relatively infrequent times to adjust the basic type of dividend policy for fundamental changes in the capital-funds needs. Then, we utilize the relevancy theory, at least in a negative form, by assuming no changes in the policy should be made without some fundamental need because of the potential adverse effects on the investors and the stock price.

Let's explore this compromise or synthesis. No change in the dividend policy means no signals are communicated to the shareholders. The low-dividend policy for growth-oriented, capital gains-seeking shareholders, or the high-dividend policy for income-oriented, dividend yield-seeking shareholders, is being maintained. Then no changes in shareholder investments are required, at least not as a result of the dividend policy. From the shareholders' view, therefore, "no news" is probably "good news."

If, however, the fundamental characteristics of the business change, then a change in the shareholder mix is probably a good idea. At such times, major increases or decreases in dividends, or marked changes in the rate of dividend increases, will go right along with the new corporate needs.

We have seen some examples in practice, with apparent irony, where the announcement of higher dividend levels has triggered a decline in the stock price. There are probably two reasons for such a phenomenon.

First, for high-growth companies, especially those with heavy research and development activities, the desire to pay more dividends may indicate a lack of growth opportunities from new products that are available to management.

Second, in addition to any reduced value from lower growth in future dividend/liquidation potential, higher dividend yield will cause some sell-off by capital gains-oriented investors. Taxes on capital gains are usually both lower than taxes on dividends (from the deduction of the original cost basis) and deferred. This allows returns to be earned on the total value rather than that value reduced by immediate taxes on current dividend payments. While some dividend yield investors may certainly be enticed to become new shareholders, there may be a stock-price decline during the transition period.

Specific Approach and Steps to Use

In conclusion, therefore, we recommend the following approach be used to establish and alter the dividend policy of a company:

1. De-emphasize the dividend policy itself, as opposed to the changes in the policy.
2. Make any changes in dividend policy infrequently, because "no news is good news," and this will avoid continued changes and confusion of the shareholders.
   - Vary debt levels to fund dividends, along with other financial needs, when a temporary shortage of cash exists. If the relevant debt/capital or interest-coverage ratios are adversely affected too

much, then do not be afraid to issue new stock to cover the temporary shortfall.

- Utilize stock repurchases when excess cash temporarily exists.

3. When the fundamental, long-term capital needs of the business change, make a fundamental alteration in the level of dividends.

- Increase dividends when long-term growth or reinvestment opportunities diminish.

- Decrease dividends, or at least the rate of dividend increase, when new growth opportunities or reinvestment requirements are uncovered.

Summary and Conclusions

The dividend policy should be planned on the basis of the type of the company and should be understood by shareholders. A capital-intensive, high-growth, and high-opportunity company may pay less in dividends or no dividends and vice versa. Another factor is consistency. Therefore, changes in dividend policy should be avoided unless there are really new corporate needs for long-term capital.

SELECTED BIBLIOGRAPHY

Chapter 1

Donaldson, G., 1963, "Financial Goals: Management vs. Stockholders," *Harvard Business Review*, Vol. 41, pp. 116–129.

Durand, D., 1959, "The Cost of Capital, Corporate Finance, and the Theory of Investment: Comment," *American Economic Review*, Vol. 49, pp. 639–655.

Fama, Eugene F., and Merton H. Miller, *The Theory of Finance*, Holt, Rinehart, and Winston, New York, NY, 1972.

Jensen, Michael C., and William H. Mecking, 1976, "Theory of the Firm: Managerial Behavior, Agency Costs and Ownership Structure," *Journal of Finance Economics*, Vol. 3, pp. 305–360.

Pogue, Gerald A., and Kishore Lall, "Corporate Finance: An Overview," *Sloan Management Review*, Spring 1974, pp. 19–38.

Chapter 2

Black, E., M. Jensen and M. Scholes, 1972, "The Capital Asset Pricing Model: Some Empirical Results," in: M. Jensen, ed., *Studies in the Theory of Capital Markets*, Praeger, New York, NY, 1972.

Fama, Eugene F., 1970, "Efficient Capital Markets: A Review of Theory and Empirical Work," *Journal of Finance*, Vol. 25, pp. 383–417.

Hayes, S. L., "The Transaction of Investment Banking," *Harvard Business Review* (January/February 1979), pp. 153–170.

Jensen, Michael C., ed., *Studies in the Theory of Capital Markets,* Praeger, New York, NY, 1972.

Rose, Peter, and Donald R. Fraser, *Financial Institutions*, Business Publications, Dallas, TX, 1980.

Van Horne, James C., *Financial Market Rates and Flows,* Prentice-Hall, Englewood Cliffs, NJ, 1978.

Chapter 3

Fama, Eugene F., and Merton H. Miller, *The Theory of Finance*, New York, NY, 1972.

Francis, Jack C., *Investments: Analysis and Management,* McGraw-Hill, New York, NY, 1980.

Francis, Jack Clark, and Dexter R. Rowell, "A Simultaneous Equation Model of the Firm for Financial Analysis and Planning," *Financial Management*, Spring 1978, pp. 29–44.

Hamada, R.S., "Portfolio Analysis, Market Equilibrium, and Corporate Finance," *Journal of Finance*, Vol. 24 (March 1969), pp. 13–22.

Hirshleifer, J., *Investment, Interest, and Capital,* Prentice-Hall, Englewood Cliffs, NJ, 1970.

Pogue, Gerald A., and Kishore Lall, "Corporate Finance: An Overview," *Sloan Management Review*, Spring 1974, pp. 19–38.

Chapter 4

Bowman, R. G., "The Theoretical Relationship between Systematic Risk and Financial (Accounting) Variables," *Journal of Finance*, Vol. 24 (June 1979), pp. 617–630.

Kim, H., 1978, "A Mean-Variance Theory of Optimal Capital Structure and Corporate Dept Capacity," *Journal of Finance*, Vol. 33, pp. 45–64.

Williams, John Burr, *The Theory of Investment Value,* Harvard University Press, Cambridge, MA, 1938.

Chapter 5

Bailey, A.D., and D. L. Jensen, "General Price Level Adjustment in the Capital Budgeting Decision," *Financial Management*, Vol. 6 (Spring 1977), pp. 26–32.

Bower, Richard S., and J. M. Jenks, "Divisional Screening Rates," *Financial Management*, Vol. 4 (Autumn 1975), pp. 42–49.

Bowman, R. G., "The Theoretical Relationship between Systematic Risk and Financial (Accounting) Variables," *Journal of Finance*, Vol. 24 (June 1979), pp. 617–630.

Kim, H., "A Mean-Variance Theory of Optimal Capital Structure and Corporate Dept Capacity," *Journal of Structure and Corporate Dept Capacity*," *Journal of Finance*, Vol. 33 (1978), pp. 45–64.

Salomon Brothers, *Supply and Demand for Credit*, Salomon Brothers, New York Plaza, New York, NY.

Van Horne, James C., *Financial Market Rates and Flows*, Prentice-Hall, Englewood Cliffs, NJ, 1978.

Chapter 6

Dewing, Arthur, *The Financial Policy of Corporations*, Ronald Press, New York, NY, 1919, 1953.

Donaldson, Gordon, "Financial Goals: Management versus Stockholders," *Harvard Business Review*, Vol. 41 (May-June 1963), pp. 116–129.

Maier, Steven F., and James H. Vander Weide, "A Practical Approach to Short-Run Financial Planning," *Financial Management*, Vol. 7 (Winter 1978), pp. 10–16.

Chapter 7

Brown, Lawrence D., and Michael S. Roseff, "The Superiority of Analyst Forecasts as a Measure of Expectations: Evidence From Earnings," *Journal of Finance*, Vol. 33 (March 1978), pp. 1–15.

Gordon, Myron J., and Eli Shapiro, "Capital Equipment Analysis: The Required Rate of Profit," *Management Science* (October 1956), pp. 102–110.

Rosenberg, Barr, and James Guy, "Bets and Investment Fundamentals," *Financial Analysts' Journal*, Vol. 32 (May-June 1976), pp. 60–72.

Wallace, Anise, "Is Beta Dead?," *Institutional Investor*, Vol. 14 (July 1980), pp. 23–30.

Chapter 8

Aaron, H., "Inflation and the Income Tax," *American Economic Review*, Vol. 66, 1976, pp. 193–199.

Asquith, Paul, "Merger Bids, Uncertainty, and Stockholder Returns," *Journal of Financial Economics*, Vol. 11, 1974.

Asquith, Paul, and E. Han Kim, "The Impact of Merger Bids on the Participating Firm Security Returns," *Journal of Finance,* Vol. 37 (December 1982), pp. 1209–1228.

Benston, George J., *Conglomerate Mergers: Causes, Consequences, and Remedies*, American Enterprise Institute for Public Policy Research, Washington, DC, 1980.

Fama, E., and G. W. Schwert, "Asset Returns and Inflation," *Journal of Financial Economics* (1977), pp. 115–146.

Mandelker, G., "Risk and Return: The Case of Merging Firms," *Journal of Financial Economics*, Vol. 1 (1974), pp. 303–336.

Manne, Henry, "Mergers and the Market for Corporate Control," *Journal of Political Economy*, Vol. 74 (1965), pp. 110–120.

Miller, Merton H., "Debt and Taxes," *Journal of Finance*, Vol. 32, May 1977, pp. 261–276.

Reids, S., *Mergers, Managers, and the Economy*, McGraw-Hill, New York, NY, 1968.

Chapter 9

Bierman, Harold, Jr., and Seymour Smidt, *The Capital Budgeting Decision, 4th ed.*, Macmillan, New York, NY, 1975.

Crum, R., and F. D. J. Derkinderen, eds., *Readings in Strategies for Corporate Investments,* Pitman, New York, NY, 1980.

Francis, Jack C., *Investments: Analysis and Management,* McGraw-Hill, New York, NY, 1980.

Levy, Hain, and Marshall Sarnant, *Capital Investment and Financial Decisions,* Prentice-Hall, Englewood Cliffs, NJ, 1978.

Miller, Merton H., and Daniel Orr, "A Model of the Demand for Money by Firms," *Quarterly Journal of Economics*, Vol. 80 (August 1966), pp. 413–435.

Osteryoung, Jarme, *Capital Budgeting: Long-Term Asset Selection*, Grid, Columbus, OH, 1974.

Reilly, Frank K., *Investment Analysis: Portfolio Management*, The Dryden Press, Hinsdale, IL, 1979.

Sharpe, William F., *Investments*, Prentice-Hall, Englewood Cliffs, NJ, 1981.

Chapter 10

Bacon, Peter W., "The Evaluation of Mutually Exclusive Investments," *Financial Management*, Summer 1977, pp. 55–58.

Bierman, Harold, Jr., and Seymour Smidt, *The Capital Budgeting Decision*, 4th ed., Macmillan, New York, NY, 1975.

Hirshleifer, Jack, "On the Theory of Optimal Investment Decision," *Journal of Political Economy*, Vol. 66, 1958, pp. 329–352.

Kummer, D., and R. Hoffmeister, "Valuation Consequences of Cash Tender Offers," *Journal of Finance*, Vol. 33, 1978, pp. 505–516.

Levy, Haim, and Marshall Sarnat, *Capital Investment and Financial Decisions*, Prentice-Hall, Englewood Cliffs, NJ, 1978.

Myers, S. C., "Interactions of Corporate Financing and Investment Decisions—Implications for Capital Budgeting," *Journal of Finance*, Vol. 29 (March 1974), pp. 1–25.

Myers, S. C., and S. M. Turnbull, "Capital Budgeting and the Capital Asset Pricing Model: Good News and Bad News," *Journal of Finance*, Vol. 32, 1977, pp. 321–333.

Osteryoung, Jarome, *Capital Budgeting: Long-Term Asset Selection*, Grid, Columbus, OH, 1974.

Sharpe, William F., "Capital Asset Prices: A Theory of Market Equilibrium under Conditions of Risk," *Journal of Finance*, September 1964, pp. 425–442.

Chapter 11

Aliber, Robert Z., *Exchange Risk and Corporate International Finance*, Wiley, New York, NY, 1978.

Dufey, Gunter, and Ian Giddy, *The International Money Market*, Prentice-Hall, Englewood Cliffs, NJ, 1978.

Eiteman, David, and Arthur Stonehill, *Multinational Business Finance, 3rd ed.*, Addison-Wesley Publishing, Reading, MA, 1982.

Lessard, Donald R., ed., *International Financial Management, Theory and Application*, Warren, Gorham & Larmont, New York, NY, 1979.

Oblak, David J., and Roy J. Helm, Jr., "Survey and Analysis of Capital Budgeting Methods Used by Multinationals," *Financial Management*, Vol. 9 (Winter 1980), pp. 37–41.

Rodriguez, Rita M., and F. Eugene Carter, *International Financial Management, 2nd ed.*, Prentice-Hall, Englewood Cliffs, NJ, 1979.

Severn, Alan K., and David R. Meister, "The Use of Multicurrency Financing by the Financial Manager," *Financial Management*, Vol. 7 (Winter 1978), pp. 45–53.

Shapiro, Alan C., "Capital Budgeting for the Multinational Corporation," *Financial Management*, Vol. 7 (Spring 1978), pp. 7–16.

Chapter 12

Brown, Lawrence D., and Michael S. Rozeff, "The Superiority of Analyst Forecasts as a Measure of Expectations: Evidence From Earnings," *Journal of Finance*, Vol. 33 (March 1978), pp. 1–15.

Chapter 13

Baxter, Nevins, "Leverage, Risk of Ruin, and the Cost of Capital," *Journal of Finance*, Vol. 22 (1967), pp. 395–404.

Caks, John, "Corporate Debt Decisions: A New Analytical Framework," *Journal of Finance*, Vol. 33 (December 1978), pp. 1297–1315.

Myers, Stewart C., "Determinants of Corporate Borrowing," *Journal of Financial Economics*, Vol. 5 (November 1977), pp. 147–175.

Silvers, J. B., "Liquidity, Risk, and Duration Patterns in Corporate Financing," *Financial Management*, Vol. 5 (Autumn 1976), pp. 54–64.

Chapter 14

Aliber, Robert Z., *Exchange Risk and Corporate International Finance*, Wiley, New York, NY, 1978.

Calderon-Rossell, Jorge R., "Covering Foreign Exchange Risks of Single Transactions," *Financial Management*, Vol. 8 (Autumn 1979), pp. 78–85.

Eiteman, David, and Arthur Stonehill, *Multinational Business Finance, 3rd ed.*, Addison-Wesley Publishing, Reading, MA, 1982.

Eliot, J. W., "The Expected Return to Equity and International Asset Prices," *Journal of Financial and Quantitative Analysis*, Vol. 13 (December 1978).

Feiger, George, and Bettrand Jacquillat, "Currency Option Bonds, Puts and Calls on Spot Exchange and the Hedging of Contingent Foreign Earnings," *Journal of Finance*, Vol. 34 (December 1979), pp. 1129–1139.

Folks, Williams R., Jr., "Decision Analysis for Exchange Risk Management," *Financial Management*, Vol. 1 (Winter 1972), pp. 101–112.

Lessard, Donald R., ed., *International Financial Management, Theory and Application*, Warren, Gorham & Larmont, New York, NY, 1979.

Naidu, G. N., and Tai Shin, "Effectiveness of Currency Futures Market in Hedging Foreign Exchange Risk," *Management International Review*, Vol. 21, No. 4 (1981), pp. 5–16.

Rodriquez, Rita M., and F. Eugene Carter, *International Financial Management*, Prentice-Hall, Englewood Cliffs, NJ, 1979.

Severn, Alan K., and David R. Meister, "The Use of Multicurrency Financing by the Financial Manager," *Financial Management*, Vol. 7 (Winter 1978), pp. 45–53.

Shapiro, Alan C., *Multinational Financial Management*, Allyn and Bacon, Boston, MA, 1982.

Chapter 15

Durand, David, "Cost of Debt and Equity Funds for Business: Trends and Problems of Measurement," Conference on Research in Business Finance, National Bureau of Economic Research, New York, NY, 1952.

Ferri, Michael G., "An Empirical Examination of the Determinations of Bond Yield Spread," *Financial Management*, Vol. 27 (Autumn 1978), pp. 40–46.

Fisher, Irving, *The Theory of Interest*, Macmillan, New York, NY, 1930.

Fisher, Lawrence, and James H. Lories, "Rates of Return on Investments in Common Stock," *Journal of Business*, Vol. 37 (1964), pp. 1–21.

Hertz, David B., "Risk Analysis in Capital Investments," *Harvard Business Review* (January–February 1964), pp. 95–106.

Modigliani, Franco, and Merton H. Miller, "The Cost of Capital, Corporation Finance and the Theory of Investment," *American Economic Review*, Vol. 48 (June 1958), pp. 261–297.

Chapter 16

Alberts, W. W., and S. H. Archer, ''Some Evidence on the Effect of Company Size on the Cost of Equity Capital,'' *Journal of Financial and Quantitative Analysis*, Vol. 8 (March 1973), pp. 229–242.

Beranek, William, ''The Weighted Average Cost of Capital and Shareholder Wealth Maximization,'' *Journal of Financial and Quantitative Analysis*, March 1977, pp. 17–32.

Chen, Andrew, ''Recent Developments in the Cost of Debt Capital,'' *Journal of Finance*, June 1978, pp. 863–883.

Durand, David, ''Cost of Debt and Equity Funds for Business: Trends and Problems of Measurement,'' Conference on Research in Business Finance, National Bureau of Economic Research, New York, NY, 1952.

Hertz, David B., ''Risk Analysis in Capital Investments,'' *Harvard Business Review* (January–February 1964), pp. 95–106.

Merton, Robert, ''On the Pricing of Corporate Debt, the Risk Structure of Interest Rates,'' *Journal of Finance* (May 1974), pp. 449–470.

Sharpe, William, 1964, ''Capital Asset Prices: A Theory of Market Equilibrium under Conditions of Risks,'' *Journal of Finance*, Vol. 19, pp. 425–442.

Chapter 17

Aggarwal, Raj Kumar, *The Management of Foreign Exchange: Optimal Policies of a Multinational Company*, Arno Press, New York, NY, 1980.

Aliber, Robert Z., *Exchange Risk and Corporate International Finance*, Wiley, New York, NY, 1978.

Calderon-Rossell, Jorge R., ''Covering Foreign Exchange Risks of Single Transactions,'' *Financial Management*, Vol. 8 (Autumn 1979), pp. 78–85.

Dufey, Gunter, and Ian Giddy, *The International Money Market*, Prentice-Hall, Englewood Cliffs, NJ, 1978.

Eiteman, David, and Arthur Stonehill, *Multinational Business Finance, 3rd ed.*, Addison-Wesley Publishing, Reading, MA, 1982.

Feiger, George, and Bettrand Jacquillat, ''Currency Option Bonds, Puts and Calls on Spot Exchange and the Hedging of Contingent Foreign Earnings,'' *Journal of Finance*, Vol. 34 (December 1979), pp. 1129–1139.

Folks, William R., Jr., and Ramesh Adrani, "Raising Funds with Foreign Currency," *Financial Executive*, Vol. 48 (February 1980), pp. 44–49.

Hayes, Douglas A., *Bank Lending Policies, Domestic and International*, Bureau of Business Research, University of Michigan, Ann Arbor, MI, 1971.

Lessard, Donald R., ed., *International Financial Management, Theory and Application*, Warren, Gorham & Larmont, New York, NY, 1979.

Naidu, G. N., "How to Reduce Transaction Exposure in International Lending," *The Journal of Commercial Bank Lending*, Vol. 63 (June 1981), pp. 39–46.

Rodriguez, Rita M., and F. Eugene Carter, *International Financial Management*, Prentice-Hall, Englewood Cliffs, NJ, 1979.

Severn, Alan K., and David R. Meister, "The Use of Multicurrency Financing by the Financial Manager," *Financial Management*, Vol. 7 (Winter 1978), pp. 45–53.

Shapiro, Alan C., *Multinational Financial Management*, Allyn and Bacon, Boston, MA, 1982.

Chapter 18

Alexander, Gordon J., "The Effect of Forced Conversions on Common Stock Prices," *Financial Management*, Vol. 9 (Spring 1980), pp. 39–45.

Alexander, Gordon J., and Roger D. Stover, "Pricing in the New Issues Convertible Debt Market," *Financial Management*, Vol. 6 (Fall 1977), pp. 35–39.

Alexander, Gordon J., and Roger D. Stover, "Market Timing Strategies in Convertible Debt Financing," *Journal of Finance*, Vol. 34 (March 1979), pp. 143–155.

Brigham, Eugene F., "An Analysis of Convertible Debentures: Theory and Some Empirical Evidence," *Journal of Finance*, Vol. 12 (March 1966), pp. 35–54.

Chapter 19

Fama, Eugene F., "The Effects of a Firm's Investment and Financing Decisions on the Welfare of Its Security Holders," *American Economic Review*, Vol. 68 (1978), pp. 272–284.

Lorie, James, and Leonard Savage, "Three Problems in Rationing Capital," *Journal of Business*, Vol. 28 (1955), pp. 229–239.

Modigliani, F., and Milton Miller, "The Cost of Capital, Corporation Finance, and the Theory of Investment," *American Economic Review*, Vol. 47, June 1958, pp. 261–297.

Myers, S. C., *A Note on the Determinants of Corporate Debt Capacity, Working Paper*, London Graduate School of Business Studies, London, England, 1975.

Chapter 20

Chen, A., and H. Kim, "Theories of Corporate Debt Policy: A Synthesis," *Journal of Finance*, Vol. 34, pp. 371–384.

Merton, R., "On the Pricing of Corporate Debt: The Risk Structure of Interest Rates," *Journal of Finance*, Vol. 29 (1974), pp. 449–470.

Miller, Merton, "Debt and Taxes," *Journal of Finance*, Vol. 32 (1977), pp. 261–276.

Myers, Stewart C., "Determinants of Corporate Borrowing," *Journal of Financial Economics*, Vol. 5 (November 1977), pp. 147–175.

Percival, J., *Risky Corporate Debt in a Market Model Context*, University of Pennsylvania, Philadelphia, PA, 1973.

Chapter 21

Black, Fisher, "Capital Market Equilibrium with Restricted Borrowing," *Journal of Business*, Vol. 45, 1972, pp. 444–455.

Masulis, R. W., "The Effects of Capital Structure Change Structure on Security Prices: A Study of Exchange Offers," Study Center in Management Economics and Finance, U.C.L.A., December 1978.

Merton, R. C., "On the Pricing of Corporate Debt: The Risk Structure of Interest Rates," *Journal of Finance*, Vol. 29 (1974), pp. 449–470.

Miller, Danny, "Common Syndrome of Business Failure," *Business Horizontal*, December 1977, pp. 43–53.

Ross, Stephen A., "The Determinants of Financial Structure: The Incentive Signaling Approach," *Bell Journal of Economics*, Vol. 8, pp. 23–40.

Chapter 22

Aggarwal, Raj, "International Differences in Capital Structure Norms," *Management International Review*, Vol. 21, No. 1 (1981), pp. 75–88.

Aggarwal, Raj Kumar, *The Management of Foreign Exchange: Optimal Policies of a Multinational Company*, Arno Press, New York, NY, 1980.

Aliber, Robert Z., *Exchange Risk and Corporate International Finance*, Wiley, New York, NY, 1978.

Eiteman, David, and Arthur Stonehill, *Multinational Business Finance, 3rd ed.*, Addison-Wesley Publishing, Reading, MA, 1982.

Lessard, Donald R., ed., *International Financial Management, Theory and Application*, Warren, Gorham & Larmont, New York, NY, 1979.

Shapiro, Alan C., "Financial Structure and Cost of Capital in the Multinational Corporation," *Journal of Finance and Quantitative Analysis*, Vol. 13 (June 1978), pp. 211–226.

Chapter 23

Jensen, Michael C., and William H. Meckling, "Theory of the Firm: Managerial Behavior, Agency Costs and Ownership Structure," *Journal of Financial Economics*, Vol. 3 (1976), pp. 305–360.

Lee, Wayne Y., and Henry H. Barker, "Bankruptcy Costs and the Firm's Optimal Debt Capacity: A Positive Theory of Capacity Structure," *Southern Economic Journal*, Vol. 43 (April 1977), pp. 1453–1465.

Miller, Danny, "Common Syndrome of Business Failure," *Business Horizontal* (December 1977), pp. 43–53.

Ross, Stephen A., "The Determinants of Financial Structure: The Incentive Signaling Approach," *Bell Journal of Economics*, Vol. 8 (1977), pp. 23–41.

Stiglitz, J. E., "On Some Aspects of the Pure Theory of Corporate Finance, Bankruptcies and Takeovers," *Bell Journal of Economics*, Vol. 3, pp. 458–482.

Chapter 24

Black, Fisher, "The Dividend Puzzle," *Journal of Portfolio Management*, Vol. 2 (1976), pp. 5–8.

Black, Fisher, and Myron Scholes, "The Effects of Dividend Yield and Dividend Policy on Common Stock Prices and Returns," *Journal of Financial Economics*, Vol. 1 (1974), pp. 1–22.

Brittain, J., *Corporate Dividend Policy*, Brookings Institution, Washington, DC, 1966.

Charest, G., "Dividend Information, Stock Returns and Market Efficiency II," *Journal of Financial Economics,* Vol. 6, No. 2/3 (1978), pp. 297–330.

Fama, E. F., and Babiak, H., "Dividend Policy: An Empirical Analysis," *Journal of the American Statistical Association*, Vol. 63, No. 4 (1968), pp. 1132–1161.

Gordon, Myron J., "Dividends, Earnings and Stock Prices," *Review of Economics and Statistics*, Vol. 41 (May 1959), pp. 99–105.

Lewellen, Wilbur G., Kenneth L. Stanley, Ronald C. Lease, and Gary G. Schlarbaum, "Some Direct Evidence on the Dividend Clientele Phenomenon," *Journal of Finance*, Vol. 33 (December 1978), pp. 1385–1399.

Miller, Merton H., and Franco Modigliani, "Dividend Policy, Growth, and the Valuation of Shares," *Journal of Business*, Vol. 34 (October 1961), pp. 411–433.

Miller, Merton, and Myron Scholes, "Dividend and Taxes: Some Empirical Evidence," *Journal of Political Economy*, Vol. 90 (1981), pp. 1118–1141.

The following publications have served as resources for all chapters in the book:

Block, Stanley B., and Geoffrey A. Hirt, *Foundations of Financial Management, 4th ed.,* Irwin, Homewood, IL, 1987.

Brealey, Richard, and Stewart Myers, *Principles of Corporate Finance, 2nd ed.,* McGraw-Hill, New York, NY, 1984.

Schall, Lawrence D., and Charles W. Haley, *Introduction to Financial Management, 4th ed.,* McGraw-Hill, New York, NY, 1986.

Van Horne, James C., *Financial Management and Policy, 7th ed.,* Prentice-Hall, Englewood Cliffs, NJ, 1986.

Weston, J. Fred, and Thomas E. Copeland, *Managerial Finance, 8th ed.,* The Dryden Press, Hinsdale, IL, 1986.

Index